TRANSCENDENT PARENTING

Raising Children in the Digital Age

Sun Sun Lim

OXFORD
UNIVERSITY PRESS

OXFORD
UNIVERSITY PRESS

Oxford University Press is a department of the University of Oxford. It furthers the University's objective of excellence in research, scholarship, and education by publishing worldwide. Oxford is a registered trade mark of Oxford University Press in the UK and certain other countries.

Published in the United States of America by Oxford University Press
198 Madison Avenue, New York, NY 10016, United States of America.

CIP data is on file at the Library of Congress
ISBN 978–0–19–066432–9 (pbk.)
ISBN 978–0–19–008898–9 (hbk.)

1 3 5 7 9 8 6 4 2

Paperback in printed by LSC Communications, United States of America
Hardback printed by Bridgeport National Bindery, Inc., United States of America

For Jin, Kai Ryn, and Kai Wyn

Your love transcends all

CONTENTS

ACKNOWLEDGMENTS

This is a book about parents and therefore about families, where I delve deeply into the love, care, and commitment that goes into making a family. I am truly fortunate to be a part of very many families—large and small, close to me and further afield, familiar and familial—who have nourished and mentored me as I muddle my way through life as a person, scholar, and a parent.

My quest to study technology and the family began at the Department of Communications and New Media at the National University of Singapore (NUS), also my alma mater, where I first found my footing as an academic and a professor. There, I had the precious opportunity to work with some extraordinary people whose steadfast friendship made my early days in academia fun and fortifying. Millie Rivera, Elmie Nekmat, Tracy Loh, Ganga Sasidharan, Kevin McGee, and (mum to all) Retna Muthuveloo have always been and still remain among my biggest cheerleaders. Thank you all for your honest feedback and unstinting encouragement. My deep appreciation also to goes the NUS Centre for Family and Population Research led by its Director, Professor Jean Yeung Wei-Jun. The Centre's Research

Development Grant funded my fieldwork on tablet use by families with preschool children and enabled me to quickly develop my nascent research ideas that birthed this book. Jean's keen interest in my work has also been a motivating force for me.

At my current academic home, the Singapore University of Technology and Design (SUTD), I have the privilege of serving as Head of Humanities, Arts and Social Sciences (HASS). Working with engineers and architects to shape the next-generation technologist, I am constantly reminded of the importance of research on the social impact of technology and heartened that SUTD recognizes it too. It awarded me with a generous start-up grant that funded my fieldwork on parents' use of mobile media, helping me to fully develop the concept of transcendent parenting. My stint at SUTD has been exciting and rewarding, throwing me into the deep end of all things technological, from additive manufacturing to natural language processing, from blockchain to swarm robotics.

I have made wonderful friends at SUTD whose support and companionship have been joyful, enriching, and transformative. Merci beaucoup to Roland Bouffanais, Chan Heng Chee, and Lim Seh Chun. It is also my good fortune that the incomparable Valeria Choo, Christina Koek, and Jane Zhang make HASS run like clockwork, allowing me to carve out small pockets of time to focus on research and writing. To my HASS faculty with expertise spanning the spectrum from anthropology to philosophy, bringing HASS to technologists is our shared endeavor, and I am grateful for your commitment and dedication.

My broader academic family in Singapore comprises many amazing individuals who have supported me along the way with thoughtful gestures, kind words, or a helping hand. Immense thanks go to Ang Peng Hwa, Michiel Baas, Colleen Chen, Ian Gordon, Ho Kong Chong, Jiow Hee Jhee, Angeline Khoo, Eddie Kuo, Lily Kong, Terence Lee Chek Liang, May Lwin, Tan Tai Yong, Lionel Wee, and

Brenda Yeoh. Within the policy and public education space, I have had the honor of serving on the National Youth Council, the National Committee on Youth Guidance and Rehabilitation, and, most recently, the Media Literacy Council. I thank my colleagues there for their rich insights, giving me a multifaceted perspective on issues of media, youth, and family.

Beyond Singapore, I am blessed to be part of a remarkably magnanimous community of scholars working on media, children, and the family. I have had the benefit of knowing and learning from this family of international colleagues whose pioneering scholarship and genuine interest in my concept of transcendent parenting gave me tremendous impetus to complete this manuscript. They created many opportunities for me to present and publish my ideas, helping me hone and refine them further. Heartfelt thanks to Sahara Byrne, Lynn Schofield Clark, Stephanie Hemelryk Donald, Kirsten Drotner, Kris Harrison, Renee Hobbs, Amy Jordan, Ana Jorge, Nancy Jennings, Dafna Lemish, Sonia Livingstone, Giovanna Mascheroni, Jessica Piotrowski, Cristina Ponte, and Erica Scharrer, and Michel Walrave. Dafna in particular has been caring, inspiring, and generous with her time and ideas—you are the consummate academic I aspire to be.

My other great research passion, mobile communication, has also been stoked by the foundational work of a formidable group of scholars. My immense appreciation goes out to Soontae An, Leopoldina Fortunati, Gerard Goggin, Leslie Haddon, Larissa Hjorth, Heather Horst, Klaus Bruhn Jensen, Steve Jones, Veronika Karnowski, James Katz, Rich Ling, Thilo von Pape, and Ran Wei. Mobile communication is also what binds me to my Pinoy family of talented academics—Jace Cabanes, Justine Espina-Letargo, Jonathan Corpus Ong, Rosel San Pascual, Cheryll Soriano, and Lia Uy-Tioco—no one does family quite like you do!

Special thanks are due to my multinational team of excellent research assistants: Becky Pham from Vietnam, Renae Loh Sze Ming from Singapore, and Tiffany Wei from the United States. Each of you helped make this book possible. Becky, you will always be my Beyonce, bright, bold, and boundless! I can't wait for the world to discover you and your many gifts. Much obliged too to the team at Oxford University Press, including Sarah Humphreville, Hallie Stebbins, Hannah Doyle, and Bronwyn Geyer, whose patience and professionalism helped smooth the bumpy path that is book writing. I am also indebted to the anonymous reviewers of my book proposal and the final manuscript for their penetrating comments and invaluable suggestions.

Returning of course to home, the heart and soul of parenting, my father and mother taught me what it means to love your children. Besides showering us with affection, they instilled in us resourcefulness, resilience, courage, and a zest for life. Eng, Ping, Sze, and I have been shaped by our parents' magical hands. I can only hope to continue their parenting legacy with my two exasperatingly adorable children Kai Ryn and Kai Wyn. You burst into our lives, making it explode with curiosity, laughter, smarts, and wide-eyed wonder. As you cross each milestone, Papa and Mama are filled with trepidation but admiration too.

And where would I be without my brilliant, capable, kind, and selfless husband Jin, whose wisdom and humor has seen us through our thrills and our trials, big and small. We have discovered the joys of the world together, and yes, parenting too. Your love transcends us. Thank you my love, you are more than I deserve.

Finally, I am eternally grateful to the families who let us peek into their busy lives. I hope I have given voice to the parents who shared their fears, challenges, hopes, and dreams. When all is said and done, know that you have tried your best.

TRANSCENDENT PARENTING

1

Transcendent Parenting and the Media-Rich Household

Let me begin by presenting three scenarios.

Scenario 1: A mother lovingly curates the iPad she's purchased for her 5-year-old daughter, ensuring that it contains only the educational and age-appropriate apps she has carefully selected. The little girl comes home from school one day, excitedly telling her mother to download Hungry Shark, a game she saw her friend playing on his iPad, where sharks savagely devour humans or rip off their limbs to leave a bloody trail. The mother is furious and frustrated that her efforts to manage her daughter's media diet have been marred.

Scenario 2: A mother checks the ClassDojo app that updates her on her son's activities in school. Although he had been receiving praise and Dojo points from the teacher the last couple of months, in recent weeks these rewards seemed to have evaporated. She is certain the teacher is still using the app because his classmate's mother had just shared via the WhatsApp parent group chat her delight at her daughter's rising Dojo points. Annoyed, she asks her son again, but

Transcendent Parenting. Sun Sun Lim, Oxford University Press (2020).

DOI: 10.1093/oso/9780190088989.001.0001

he is noncommittal. She resolves to write the teacher to find out if he is facing problems in school.

Scenario 3: A father berates his university-aged daughter for omitting to "like" her mother's latest Facebook post. Although the daughter is away in another country for her university education, her parents maintain close contact with her via WhatsApp and follow her Facebook and Instagram accounts to check on her. It seems that her failure to like her mother's post has led the latter to feel hurt and neglected.

I see in these scenarios the phenomenon of what I call "transcendent parenting." In many urban societies today, mobile media are increasingly pervasive, especially within the home. It is not uncommon for homes to be littered with devices, enveloping the digitally connected family within a constellation of always-on and always-on-hand mobile media. Indeed, in the "making" of family, mobile media have come to play a central role.

Young couples excitedly announce their tentative steps toward parenthood by sharing hazy ultrasound images of their as yet unnamed babies over Instagram or WeChat. The dutiful chronicling of their journey together as a family then peaks at the birth of the child, along with various other milestones such as the first day of school, losing a tooth, winning a race, and graduating high school or college. Through it all, the mobile phone is their trusty aide, helping to capture lasting memories that are showcased via social media, binding all in the family to their varied networks. These picture-perfect moments, frozen in time, bely much of the frenetic activity surrounding these significant events. Because behind the scenes of digitally connected families today are busy lifestyles lubricated by micro-coordination, with mobile phones linking parents to children as they manage hectic schedules and a slew of mobile media keeping them informed and entertained.

THE EMERGENCE OF TRANSCENDENT PARENTING

The advent of ubiquitous mobile media has enabled and engendered the practice of transcendent parenting throughout every stage of a child's development, from infancy through adolescence and all the way to early adulthood. In the wake of mobile media and cloud computing, the scope and scale of parenting obligations have broadened considerably, where each phase of the child's life introduces fresh communication opportunities as well as new challenges. Transcendent parenting has thus emerged in light of significant transformations in the mobile media landscape that allow parents to transcend many realms.

First, parents seek to **transcend the physical distance between them and their children**, exploiting the connectivity of mobile media to always be there for their children, whether to help them along or protect them from harm. The natural parental instinct and desire to shield children from adversity and risk is now more actively realized through progressively sophisticated affordances of mobile media. Webcams, CCTV (closed-circuit television) cameras, location tracking, mobile phone connections, and social media footprints offer some measure of assurance about their children's well-being. Increasingly, children who are armed with personal mobile phones are perpetually linked to their parents. They can continue to seek their parents' assistance as they independently go about their day. Even when children grow older and leave home to forge their own existence at college or at work, transcendent parenting persists where parents continue to play a key role in their children's lives because mobile media and digital communication pave the way for sustained, involved parenting. In such a climate, whether parents are at work or at home, together or apart from their children, they continue to parent. With this continual connection, their children are never far from their thoughts or concerns, and their parental presence is channeled and felt via these digital tethers.

Second, besides exercising oversight, parents also seek to socialize their children, guiding them through their interactions with peers and teachers, both online and offline. As online interactions leave a visible digital trail, parents can glean insights from their children's social media interactions to identify potential issues, offer advice, inculcate values, and nurture life skills. Face-to-face interactions can also have a digital spillover, with some parents using online platforms to ease tensions arising from offline altercations or to advocate for their children if injustice is perceived. Parents must therefore **transcend every online and offline environment their children transit through**, be the voice of reason, and provide wise counsel along the way. Although parents can do their utmost to erect a walled garden for their children at home, it is hardly impervious but always open to content streaming via the cloud, from Snapchat messages to MMORPGs games with virtual strangers (Jiow and Lim 2012). Hence, just as children's interactions with peers traverse offline spaces and online environments, parenting must transcend those realms too. Parents must thus strive to understand and even preempt children's peer interactions and climate of sociality, as well as to apprehend the roles that mobile media play in those processes. Social interactions in online channels have their own language, logics, rhythms, and norms that children may adopt and practice but without fully appreciating their implications and consequences. These wider possibilities thus raise issues that require concerted parental guidance and support. Such a responsibility necessitates that parents possess both emotional maturity and technical prowess to understand the opportunities and challenges posed by mobile media environments to engage in transcendent parenting.

Finally, beyond mobile media linking parents to children, a growing proliferation of channels allow parents to communicate with their children's caregivers, teachers, and other parents, along with platforms that directly draw parents into their children's learning. Home-school conferencing apps, parent-parent chat groups, gradebooks, and homework-helper apps enable and demand that parents be hands-on in their children's educational endeavors. Wherever parents are therefore, they are extensively and inextricably bound to their children and their needs. Transcendent parenting is thus characterized by its defiance of temporal limits. Parents must **transcend timeless time as experienced in the apparent ceaselessness of parenting duties**, where you are constantly parenting regardless of whether your child is by your side or out of sight. Castells (1996) observed that in our digitally networked society, with its unremitting information flows, we are often compelled to march to the beat of "timeless time" and mobile-connected parents seem especially vulnerable. Whereas dropping a child off at school or a playdate during the pre-mobile era afforded parents a temporary reprieve from their parenting duties, the mobile-connected parent is on permanent standby for emergency calls or routine communication from their children, and the people and organizations in whose care they are placed. Rare is the parent of today who has not received a distress text message from the school about the child or an e-mail reminder about a permission slip that must be signed and submitted. And after the children have gone to bed, parents take on the second shift (Hochschild and Machung 2012), coordinating after-school playdates, making childcare arrangements, paying for school excursions, and replying to e-mails from teachers. Transcendent parenting is therefore a state where parenting duties are on an endless loop, where parents parent relentlessly, with little or no chance of a meaningful respite.

Essentially therefore, transcendent parenting is especially pervasive in urban, middle-class societies where mobile communication is avidly used. I do not conceive of it as a form of parenting in and of itself. Instead, as I will seek to demonstrate in my upcoming chapters that transcendent parenting is enabled and exacerbated by the rising use of mobile media and is a parenting practice of the mobile age. I will also identify and explicate the key parenting priorities among Asia's urban middle class, to explain how these influence the emergence and enactment of transcendent parenting. Indeed, Asia is an expansive and diverse region and I elaborate later on which parts of Asia I refer to. But some common threads can be discerned in terms of the principal duties that society deems critical for parents to fulfill: inculcation of values in children; oversight and supervision of children to protect them from harm and adverse influence; and support of children in their academic endeavors.

My argument for transcendent parenting is grounded in the experiences of Asia's urban middle class, with Singapore as my main focus. In my subsequent chapters, I will present in-depth findings from my fieldwork in Singapore to uncover the particular ways in which transcendent parenting is emerging and discernible in urban societies that have embraced mobile media in the home and in their everyday lives. The research I mainly draw on for this book was conducted between 2016 and 2019, and I provide a more detailed description in the Appendix. At relevant junctures, I will also reference studies that I have completed across my 15 years of studying technology domestication by families and young people in Asia, where I have examined the media use of middle-class families in various countries including China, Indonesia, South Korea, and Vietnam, besides, of course, Singapore.

In many ways, Singapore presents an appropriate departure point from which to consider the phenomenon of transcendent parenting and its implications for the urban middle class. It is highly connected, and its information and communication technology infrastructure is reliable and comprehensive (Winstedt et al. 2019). Mobile and wireless broadband penetration have both reached saturation, with smartphone penetration among the highest in the world. With the arrival of mobile technology and social media, there has been a marked shift in media-content consumption habits toward online media, with youths as the most avid Internet users; mainly engaging in communication, leisure, and information-gathering activities. An urbanized city-state, the country has developed into an affluent information-based economy with world-leading trade, financial, and industrial sectors. Devoid of natural resources, the country has made sustained investments in its people through a structured and broad-ranging education system that is world renowned (Simonds 2018). In the 1980s, Singapore's then Prime Minister Lee Kuan Yew declared that Singapore was a "middle-class society" with 80% of its citizens owning the residential properties they lived in. A recent social stratification survey estimated that between 46 and 54% of Singaporeans were in the middle or higher class (Tan 2015). The country prides itself as a meritocracy, with academic achievement widely regarded as the passport to social mobility. Many Singaporean parents thus invest heavily in their children's education for enhanced cultural and social capital (Tan and Tan 2016).

MEDIA AND URBAN MIDDLE-CLASS HOUSEHOLDS IN ASIA

In most urban societies throughout the world today, middle-class households are well equipped with a plethora of mobile media devices that are used for work, education, recreation, and the micro-coordination of family schedules. In families with school-going children, this proliferation of household media devices demands that parents create optimal conditions in which these gadgets are appropriated in the domestic space. Indeed, as the family context is the child's first and primary environment for consuming media, it is critical to understand the role of media and technology in the lives of families (Jennings 2017). Parents are the principal architects when it comes to acquiring media products, devices, and services for children, setting the rules for media use and misuse, helping children navigate media environments and understand media content (Harrison 2015). Parents also play the critical role of determining the household routines in and around which media use is organized.

The urban middle-class household in Asia has become significantly infused with media devices. Device ownership, especially of mobile media devices such as smartphones and tablets, has risen across the board along with household Internet access and time spent on social media. Notably, whereas devices such as desktop computers and televisions tend to be shared communally within households, mobile media devices tend to be personally owned and individually used.

In most countries listed in Table 1.1, Internet access and social media use exceed television viewing time, thus reflecting the importance of social media as a communication platform and information source.

Although research on media use among Asia's urban middle-class families is still far from comprehensive, there has certainly been encouraging evidence of growth. In particular, more research is being conducted on households with children, and these studies span the age spectrum. For households with very young children in particular, the research indicates that mobile media devices play a prominent role. Studies of families with preschool children in Hong Kong have found that besides toys, parents of children aged 3 to 7 often used smartphones, tablets, and computers for the children's play and learning activities at home, and for family communication or entertainment purposes (Choi 2016; Wu et al. 2014). Similarly, in Singapore with children aged 7 and below, a survey found that parents appreciate touchscreen devices for their ability to enhance their children's motor, psychomotor, and sensory skills; boost intellectual development; and cultivate their emotional and artistic

Table 1.1 HOUSEHOLD MEDIA DEVICE PENETRATION AND USE IN SELECTED ASIAN COUNTRIES

Country	*Urbanization rates (% population)**	*Internet penetration rates (% of population)**	*Penetration rates of devices (% household)^*				*Average time spent with media per day**			
			Digital TVs	*Smart-phones*	*Laptops*	*Tablets*	*Internet via PC or tablet*	*Internet via mobile phone*	*Social media via any device*	*Television viewing*
China	57%	53%	73%	220%	39.5%	20.5%	6h 21m	3h 4m	1h 50m	1h 20m
Hong Kong	100%	85%	142%	810%	136%	290.0%	5h 59m	2h 26m	1h 41m	1h 38m
India	33%	35%	51.2%	107%	6.5%	3.9%	8h 0m	3h 22m	2h 36m	1h 51m
Indonesia	55%	51%	66.5%	140%	9.0%	25.0%	8h 44m	3h 55m	3h 16m	2h 23m
Japan	94%	93%	130%	161.7%	63.7%	39.6%	4h 6m	0h 57m	0h 40m	2h 15m
Malaysia	76%	71%	133.2%	278.6%	78.1%	46.1%	8h 31m	3h 43m	3h 19m	2h 4m

(*continued*)

Table 1.1 CONTINUED

Country	*Urbanization rates (% population)**	*Internet penetration rates (% of population)**	*Penetration rates of devices (% household)^*				*Average time spent with media per day**			
			Digital TVs	*Smart-phones*	*Laptops*	*Tablets*	*Internet via PC or tablet*	*Internet via mobile phone*	*Social media via any device*	*Television viewing*
Philippines	44%	58%	93%	180%	24.2%	19.0%	9h 0m	3h 36m	4h 17m	2h 30m
Singapore	100%	82%	113.4%	409.6%	105.3%	80.2%	6h 41m	2h 21m	2h 7m	1h 33m
South Korea	92%	90%	111.3%	281.2%	65.1%	41.5%	4h 54m	2h 4m	1h 11m	2h 11m
Thailand	52%	67%	114%	220%	34.5%	35.3%	8h 49m	4h 14m	2h 48m	2h 26m
Vietnam	31%	53%	108.2%	115%	28.5%	19.5%	6h 53m	2h 33m	2h 39m	1h 26m

* As of 2017, compiled from Euromonitor International, including data from trade sources and national statistics.

^ As of 2017, compiled from We Are Social's "Digital in 2017" study, including data from different data providers and surveys.

aspects (Ebbeck et al. 2016). Parents were however circumspect about adverse impacts on the children's health, including damage to eyesight, physical inactivity, addiction, exposure to inappropriate content, and stunted social and communication skills. Parallels can be drawn with a South Korean study that found that parents appreciated how touchscreen devices helped raise their children's technological skills. However, these parents were rather concerned about the negative impact of touchscreen devices on their children, including developing an unhealthy obsession, negatively impacting socioemotional development, impeding the child's creativity or liveliness, and physical damage to their eyesight and posture (Seo and Lee 2017). Parents would thus exercise restrictive mediation as many felt that touchscreens do not lend themselves well to co-using the devices with their children. This situation was mirrored in Indonesian families with children aged 2 to 7, where parents introduced smartphones and tablets to the children for educational, entertainment, and babysitting purposes but were anxious about the risks from device use such as eyestrain, sedentary lifestyles, and exposure to violence (Sekarasih 2016). As a result, the parents mainly engaged in restrictive mediation on time and accessed content.

This belief in the educational value of tablet devices is indeed salient, and there is a perception that parents let their children use mobile media devices to ensure that they do not lag behind their peers, especially as they entered primary school. A study of Singaporean parents of primary 3 children found that they supported extended use of smartphones for schoolwork at home, such as using the Internet for searching purposes and using school applications, although they expressed concerns about the children's misuse of smartphones for gaming or watching videos (Hong et al. 2016). The parents typically set time restrictions on the children's use of smartphones and the Internet, only granting access to the children after they finished their homework or for schoolwork-related use. In the same vein, a study of Indonesian parents discovered that they hold a neutral attitude toward their upper elementary school children's television watching but have a positive attitude toward their children's computer use because they wanted their children to be as tech-savvy as their peers (Hendriyani et al. 2014). Most of these Indonesian households owned multiple media devices. The parents were reported to have media-related discussions with their children about books, television, phones, computers, electronic games, and music media, with electronic games and Internet use more frequently linked to parental restrictions. Ideological beliefs did also influence parental attitudes and practices. Another Indonesian study noted that Muslim mothers in Indonesia with young children aged 8 to 10 actively managed their children's Internet access and consumption based on Islamic principles (Rahayu and Lim 2016). The more religious families strived to strengthen their children's faith as a bulwark against un-Islamic Internet content. The less religious families perceived the Internet as more beneficial and welcomed rather than resisted such technology use.

As children enter high school and beyond, mobile media play an even greater role in their lives, and even though their parents attempt to exercise mediation, these young people are independent enough to circumvent any restrictions. One Chinese study found that parents in China emphasized the importance of education and perceived mobile phones, the Internet, gaming, and social media to be distractions to their middle school children's academic achievements, so they limited the children's phone use (McDonald 2016). However, the children found creative means to circumvent parental restrictions. Separately, trans-local families with children studying in universities in Shanghai used WeChat to communicate and receive each other's location information through posts with marked locations or clues to locations via photos, which enabled the parents to monitor their children's movements in an "intimate, yet not invasive manner" and to have more topics to talk about (Hjorth et al. 2016, 151). The children, however, negotiated such online connections sometimes by self-censoring before posting messages, selectively sharing with their parents, or blocking their parents for a while and then adding them back. This study finds resonance with another I conducted on Indonesian and Vietnamese university students in Singapore where we noted that their parents would observe their social media activity to find out how their children were faring overseas (Lim and Pham 2016).

Overall, mobile media perform a critical role in the everyday lives of these middle-class families in Asia, offering a multitude of educational, recreational, and communicative possibilities to families with children across the age spectrum. The families' domestication of mobile media is shaped by their perceptions of these technologies and the values that underpin their familial relationships.

MEDIA USE THROUGHOUT THE CHILD'S LIFE

If we ask parents today where their children consume media, a likely answer would be "anywhere and everywhere!" As unhelpful as this answer may seem, it nonetheless captures the reality for young people around the world who enjoy access to a widening plethora of mobile media devices (Ling and Bertel 2013). It is not uncommon for households with even very young children to be littered with media devices, where besides mainstays such as televisions and desktop computers, portable ones abound in the form of smartphones, tablet computers, video games, and music players. In such an environment, media use often constitutes the main activity of children at various junctures throughout the day and as "filler" activities in the interstices of their daily lives. Furthermore, multiscreen practices are increasingly the norm across all age groups, such as playing on a tablet computer while watching television, or messaging friends on the mobile phone while surfing the Internet on a laptop. Of course, the nature of mobile media use varies with age and is markedly influenced by the trend toward young people's personal possession of these devices and the intensifying media use that results. This growing prevalence of mobile media devices, many of which are equipped with Internet connectivity, has distinct implications for young people at every stage of their development.

For younger children, the day will often include media activities such as watching television and playing video games at home, interspersed with outdoor excursions that may involve music, videos, or games on mobile devices. Preschoolers usually have minimal control over the media devices and content they can access. Hence, parents of preschoolers play an especially critical role in building and landscaping the child's media environment. For mobile devices, this would include purchasing a gadget that they consider appropriate; downloading suitable apps, games, and videos; and perhaps setting up parental control filters to prevent the child from chancing upon harmful or unsavory content. The relentless innovation in apps for children also imposes on parents the tasks of keeping up with the latest offerings and being able to judge potential benefits and harms. To promote children's engagement with more positive media content, parents may actively curate household devices with apps, content, and channels they deem advantageous for their children's development. They may also engage in active co-viewing or co-use where they guide their children on their media consumption, in the hope that they will learn to make wise choices. For kids of preschool age therefore, parents play an important role in managing the child's media diet.

As children advance to primary school age, they will enjoy some degree of independence from their parents, perhaps traveling to school on their own and interacting with friends in or after school.

In such settings, children with their own mobile devices are likely to whip them out, and shared media use among the children may occur by, for example, watching a video on a phone or playing tablet games together. While these interactions are likely to be innocuous, exposure to age-inappropriate content such as pornography or violent games may occur via such shared media use. After all, parenting values and standards differ and not all parents are equally motivated about regulating media content—what is acceptable in one household may be anathema to another. More vigilant parents would then realize that short of ensconcing their children in a bubble, the only way for them to safeguard their children against incidental exposure to inappropriate content is to instill in them values and skills of discernment.

Besides matters relating to the child's own media consumption, mobile media have also heralded new parenting obligations in the child's younger years. Now that schools have a direct connection to parents via their mobile phones, they frequently communicate their requests and instructions directly to parents, rather than via the child with a note from the teacher. Schools are increasingly utilizing home-school conferencing apps to send parents personalized circulars, exam grades, and assignment deadlines. On their part, parents have also taken it upon themselves to create message groups for all the parents in, say, a kindergarten class or playgroup. Typically set up on platforms such as WhatsApp or Facebook, such groups facilitate parent-to-parent sharing of information pertaining to homework, school-related activities, as well as social events involving their children. While such channels of communication are in many ways a boon, enabling the parent to keep abreast of opportunities that can enhance the child's academic and social development, it adds yet another responsibility to the long list of parenting tasks that must be attended to.

With older children aged 12–16, who are likely to have their own media devices, the situation becomes even more fluid and complex. Compared to their younger counterparts whose physical whereabouts are more closely managed by parents, this group enjoys considerable autonomy. As they leave the house for school or social gatherings, they are likely to carry their own mobile phone as well as maybe a tablet, portable game device, or laptop computer. They would also have their own social media accounts that they use to connect with friends and family. Being older, they possess a broader range of online skills and therefore are able to surf the Internet unassisted, and to download apps or games, as well as to upload content of their own creation.

Parents need to therefore view their children as social actors, media consumers, and content creators. Parents who wish to mediate their children's online social experiences have to consider the varieties of spaces their children can enter and explore of their own accord, the kinds of social interaction they may engage in, and the people whom they could possibly encounter. Face-to-face socializing with peers is increasingly supplemented by mediated interactions via social media platforms such as WhatsApp, Instagram, and Snapchat. Such mediated interactions with peers can be convenient, enjoyable, and fun. However, although children have the technological competency to communicate through these services, they lack the emotional maturity to deal with communication situations that are awkward or difficult. For example, an argument that escalates within a group chat may fracture friendships and create unwelcome strains, possibly precipitating into online indiscretions and cyberbullying that affect their offline interactions as well. In the case of interactions with unknown online acquaintances, some of whom can be of a distinctly different sociocultural makeup, children need to be prepared for encounters with people whose behavior, values, and worldviews may not resonate with theirs.

To prime their children for such independent endeavors that are replete with benefits and risks, parents have to seriously reflect on the kinds of values they wish to instill in their children, while also walking them through different scenarios in which the child's judgment may be tested. Providing such guidance will require time and effort in self-education on the parents' part in order to acquaint themselves with the complex online environment and the ever-growing range of communication platforms, such as Snapchat, Instagram, and TikTok, each of which presents different affordances and challenges. Some parents may also seek to impose rules and restrictions such as prohibiting the exploration of particular sites or requiring that passwords be shared. Similarly, as media consumers, children are also entering unchartered terrain with content that requires parental interpretation and scaffolding. The exploding universe of user-generated, multimodal, and genre-defying content can be stimulating but also confusing and trying for children's critical capacities. Finally, as content creators, children may derive gratifications from producing and sharing blogs, photos, videos, and more but are less attuned to issues of privacy protection, online victimization, reputation management, and intellectual property. Again, there is an expectation for parents to intervene to prevent their children from putting themselves in vulnerable and risky positions.

In late adolescence, parents are likely to loosen the apron strings further and to vest trust and individual responsibility in the child. By this age, it would be less a matter of instilling values in their children and more of reinforcing those already inculcated in their earlier years. As the child matures, the parent-child relationship is also likely to transition away from a superior-subordinate nature toward more of a buddy or peer dynamic. However, this does not relieve the parent of having to offer guidance and support for the child's mobile media use. As the child's personal tastes and preferences in media content would already be fairly developed, parents may only need to weigh in occasionally on controversial content or difficult situations. Parents are more likely to have to grapple with issues of managing excessive use and ensuring that the child's attachment to mobile media devices does not compromise his/her overall well-being and relationships with significant others (Kwon et al. 2013).

With entry into emerging adulthood, young people will enjoy an unprecedented degree of personal independence. Those who are bound for tertiary education will leave home for the first time to live on their own and be responsible for their personal needs and routines. And yet, even if they are no longer in proximity to their parents, there is growing evidence that these young people are keeping in intermittent contact with their parents via mobile communication (see for example Gentzler et al. 2011; Hjorth et al. 2016). These would include text messages, voice and video calls, and social media connections exchanged on a regular basis. My recent research on Vietnamese university students in Singapore shows that even when the students hail from semi-rural areas where household Internet connectivity is not the norm, they set up Internet-enabled mobile phone subscriptions for their parents back home to ensure a constant line of contact with their parents (Pham and Lim 2016). Members of these transnational families then communicate frequently using affordable and visually rich messaging platforms, such as Skype or LINE, that allow for voice and text communication. Despite being separated by vast distances, the parents continue to check on the safety and whereabouts of their children by contacting them directly or by viewing their social media updates, and, in some instances, even contacting their children's friends.

OUTLINE OF THE BOOK

My upcoming chapters will show how transcendent parenting is practiced across different phases of the child's life and how mobile media facilitate but also intensify this parenting practice. In Chapter 2, "Parenting Today," I identify key priorities among parents of Asia's urban middle-class families. I explain how they tend to focus on three main priorities: inculcating values in their children to ensure positive maturation, exercising oversight and supervision over them to protect them from harm and adverse influence, and providing support for their children's academic achievement to pave their way for future success. I also review research on the sociology of parenting to grasp the trends amidst which transcendent parenting has unfolded. Related concepts such as intensive parenting, concerted cultivation, and paranoid parenting will also be analyzed to explore how they intersect with transcendent parenting.

Thereafter, each of my chapters will focus on key realms of young people's lives including the school, the home, and the social sphere to show how mobile media are assuming a growing position in the lives of these middle-class families. The empirical evidence I draw upon to illustrate my arguments is based on interviews with 70 parents, on which I provide a description of my research method and my respondents' family profiles in the Appendix. In Chapter 3, "At Home," I discuss how parents perceive their roles as principal nurturers of their children, ensuring that they enjoy the best material conditions and socioemotional support to thrive in school. I show how these priorities also manifest themselves in parents' use of mobile media for fulfilling their parenting duties. I focus specifically on education in Chapter 4, "At School," where I reveal how mobile media are increasingly used in the service of children's academic pursuits. These can run the gamut from schools using mobile apps for home-school conferencing to parents leveraging WhatsApp chat groups and homework-helper sites to support their children's studies. I will discuss how such involvement may compound the parenting burden.

In Chapter 5, "Out and About," I explore parents' use of mobile media and communication to enhance their children's personal safety and their own perceptions of the same. I show how mobile media in the form of live webcam feeds and location-tracking services make it easier for parents of younger children to keep track of their children's whereabouts. I argue that even as children grow older and more independent, parental oversight persists through ever-present mobile connections between parents and their children, as well as an extended parental surveillance network. Beyond these custom apps for location monitoring, parents of teens and emerging adults are also wont to scrutinize their children's social media footprints to undertake subtle and covert remote supervision.

Chapter 6, "At Play" analyzes the realm of children's sociality, where I discuss how parents can become heavily involved in their children's peer interactions, both online and offline, especially since they are concerned about their children's contact risks. I present evidence to show how parents use the digital trail of mediated communication to gain insights into their children's social interactions to offer guidance. I also explore how such parental interventions can deny children valuable opportunities for learning to interpret social situations and to manage their online and offline personae. I conclude in Chapter 7 by explicating how mobile communication has engendered the conditions for transcendent parenting practices to emerge, thereby transforming family life. I then expound on why and in what ways the concept of transcendent parenting is relevant to urban middle-class societies in other parts of the world. Finally, I contemplate the mutually constitutive, spiraling relationship between mobile communication and parenting.

2

Parenting Today

It was still pitch dark when he arrived to join the queue. Yet the line of anxious parents was already snaking around the fine arts center. He couldn't believe that he woke up at 5 a.m. on a Sunday morning to get his 6-year-old daughter entry into a very exclusive ballet class. His wife had convinced him that their daughter had a natural talent for dance, and if she built up a competitive portfolio of performances, it would help her score admission into a reputable, "elite" high school. This was their backup plan for her in case she didn't do well in the crucial national exams she would take when she turned 12. He counted the number of parents in front of him and was relieved, confident that he would secure his daughter the much-coveted spot. But he began to dread the three-hour wait before the admissions office opened at 9 a.m.

As we reckon with the technological landscape that has created the conditions for transcendent parenting, what is the social climate of parenting from which transcendent parenting has emerged? To better understand the broader picture of parenting practices today, a review of dominant themes in the parenting discourse of the past few decades will help illuminate notable shifts in parenting goals and priorities over time. Given the socioeconomic background of the families I studied, I will focus my discussion on the urban middle class.

Transcendent Parenting. Sun Sun Lim, Oxford University Press (2020).

DOI: 10.1093/oso/9780190088989.001.0001

It has been observed that members of the global middle class have a somewhat uniform experience in terms of their needs, priorities, and goals. The middle class around the world seems unified by "a host of context-specific desires, aspirations, and anxieties" (Heiman, Liechty, and Freeman 2012, 20) that are reflected in their quest for lifestyles, spaces, and modes of consumption seen as synonymous with the middle-class. While "middle-classness" is often oriented toward and expressed through consumerist practices that signal class distinction, middle-class practices extend beyond consumerism. Especially with regard to families with children, a wealth of research in urban societies throughout the world reflects a shift in middle-class families toward child-centric lifestyles where children are born into smaller nuclear families that are not necessarily part of a multigenerational household structure.

Another key trend is the transformation of childhoods across modern economies worldwide, where children benefit from universal education and the effects of this "scholarization" of childhood (Waterson and Behera 2011). This translates into children spending more time being socialized in school settings, greater supervision over children's time both inside and outside the home, and a growing shift toward middle-class parents filling their children's schedules with extra tutelage and co-curricular activities, often at the expense of free, unscheduled time (Göransson 2015). Indeed, childhood thus becomes "a site of accumulation and commodification" (Katz 2008, 5) where parents engage in material acquisition and social practices that grant their children a competitive advantage over their peers. These trends are thus not unique to European or North American settings and are replicated and even intensifying in other parts of the world, especially Asia (Waterson and Behera 2011).

PARENTING DISCOURSES OVER TIME

Research on the evolution of parenting provides a useful sociological backdrop to the concept of transcendent parenting. Many concepts have been advanced, such as intensive parenting (Hays 1996), concerted cultivation (Lareau 2003), paranoid parenting (Furedi 2008), and parenting out of control (Nelson 2010), that both inform and intersect with transcendent parenting. Indeed, these concepts, although originating in the United States and Europe, have found considerable resonance in Asia. Principally, the emergence of these distinct yet related concepts signals a strong discursive momentum building around matters relating to raising children. Furedi (2002) observes that, over time, the notion that children require special care and attention has been amplified, resulting in considerable weight being placed on parenting responsibilities. Parental influence and efforts are increasingly deemed paramount in shaping children into who they are, and the adults they will become—a perspective referred to as parental determinism (Faircloth 2014). This parental determinism frame has led to greater scrutiny over parents and their duties, even though parents' ability to perfectly and successfully shape their children according to plan is far from guaranteed. Various studies have been undertaken and concepts proposed to capture parenting trends that reflect this perception of parental determinism.

In particular, the concept of intensive parenting has found resonance in many parts of the world. Parents, it is argued, are motivated by generativity to nurture the next generation (McAdams 1993), and their children's success reflects their parents' ability, thus influencing the latter's sense of self-worth and self-perception. Children are therefore not just to be birthed but also to be cultivated and groomed, often becoming a veritable exercise in self-actualization for their parents (Ungar 2007).

In her landmark work *The Cultural Contradictions of Motherhood* (1996), sociologist Sharon Hays observed that American mothers in the 1990s went well beyond performing basic parenting duties. Instead, they focused their energies principally on their children and expended significant amounts of time, effort, and material resources to nurture them. Hays noted that this approach was "child-centred, expert-guided, emotionally absorbing, labour intensive and financially expensive" (8). This approach was typically manifested as an extreme concern for providing the child with extra classes in arts, sports, personal deportment, as well as lessons that would offer them an academic advantage over their peers, even vesting them with the finest material possessions. Parents would also seek expert advice on how they should proactively build a positive relationship with their children. Although she noted that not every mother was able to meet these unyielding standards, this approach to mothering was accepted, both tacitly and explicitly, as the parenting roles to which all mothers should strive. She also noted that counterintuitively, even though more women are in the workforce, the amount of time parents spend with their children has risen, and the quality of time has grown more intense as well. This logic of intensive parenting is, as Faircloth (2014, 31) asserts, a "cultural script" or normative standard of parenting that parents feel compelled to aspire to.

Although "intensive parenting" as a phenomenon was identified by Sharon Hays two decades ago, it remains highly relevant today. More recently, Margaret Nelson's *Parenting out of Control* (2010), also set in the United States, extended the focus on parental involvement in young people's lives when she showed that parents exercise "hyper vigilance" over their children by utilizing technological aids such as baby monitors and mobile phones to keep tabs on their well-being. She noted that such parental vigilance originates during the child's infancy and is sustained all the way to college, with some parents even bunking in with their children in the college dorms during the first week of school.

More recently, also arguing from a study in the United States, Annette Lareau's work, *Unequal Childhoods: Race, Class and Family Life* (2003), introduced the concept of "concerted cultivation" that relates to intensive parenting. She argues that compared to poor and working-class parents, middle-class parents are more adept at navigating the education system and harness their considerable social capital and material resources to be more involved in their children's school lives, thereby conferring greater advantage to their children. They also teach their children to be more assertive and conscious of their rights, and to acquire speech and behavior that will enable them to integrate well into social networks and institutions. She notes that, as a consequence, middle-class children are more confident but possibly more entitled as well. Concerted cultivation thus appears to be yet another variant of intensive parenting, necessitating significant involvement by parents in nurturing their children. By the same token, Shaw (2008) found that even in their leisure patterns, families seek activities that can best enhance children's health and well-being. Similarly, Wolf (2010) writes of "total" motherhood where mothers are expected to be authorities on all aspects of mothering, serving as de facto "lay paediatricians, psychologists, consumer products safety inspectors, toxicologists, and educators" (xv) so that they can mind their children to the best of their abilities. Motherhood is thus consummately child-centered, with a mother's personal needs neglected and costs to her selfhood disregarded. Indeed, criticisms of intensive parenting practices tend to dwell on the adverse effects on children, without consideration for the costs to the parents in terms of their own time, emotional investment, and self-actualization (Bristow 2014).

Another significant thread in treatises on parenting comprises concepts that delve into the negative impact that more intensive parenting approaches can have on children. These concepts tend to employ value-laden terms such as paranoid parenting, overprotective parenting, hyperparenting, and helicopter parenting.

In Frank Furedi's book *Paranoid Parenting* (2008), he deems as exceedingly unhealthy the turn toward parental determinism and over-inflation of childhood vulnerability. He argues that such perspectives place too much stock in parents' abilities to determine the course of their children's development, while underestimating children's resilience, thereby encouraging and justifying excessive parental interference. By extension, parental supervision is always seen as an unequivocal virtue and must be maintained whether directly or through vicarious means. As a consequence, he argues that parenting has become overly burdensome, thus deterring couples from having children. He refers to the confluence of these trends as a "culture of paranoid parenting" where every aspect of a child's life is seen to be fraught with risk, and parents must therefore seek expert guidance on how best to raise their children to ameliorate such risks. He contends that parents have become increasingly insecure and uncertain about their parenting abilities and are consequently more susceptible to inflated risk assessments from purported experts. He cautions that while the media is always fingered as the culprit in propagating paranoid parenting practices, it is simply reflecting societal concerns that have developed on the backs of risk entrepreneurs and "an industry of advice providers" (58). With childbirth for example, parents are confronted with a vast array of books, magazines, videos, and other media content proffering advice on successful childrearing.

Beyond childbirth, he observes that the role of the parent as determined by societal expectations has also expanded significantly. "The roles of the modern parent stretch from that of a chauffeur, who transports the kids from one activity to another, to an educator, who supplements formal schooling" (Furedi 2008, 71). Indeed, he notes the situation in the West that schools and school-related responsibilities have dominated a growing share of parents' time. There is a growing valorization of parental involvement in children's education, encouraged by the pronouncements of politicians, educators, and childrearing experts. "The expansion of parental responsibility in children's schooling represents a major claim on their time and energies. But adding yet another load on the backs of parents is unlikely to improve the quality of their children's education" (88). Furedi asserts, therefore, that there is a "parenting time famine" (90) that imposes considerable pressure on parents. Yet it is rarely discussed in public even if acutely felt in private, and that "the real issue is not time in the abstract but the culturally endorsed redefinition of parenting time" (97). He further argues that parenting has become a competitive sport where parents feel anxious to outdo or at least keep up with their peers in nurturing their children. Such competitive pressures then lead to hyperparenting practices.

Given the heightened concerns about the apparent emergence of hyperparenting, some researchers have sought to empirically assess such trends. Ungar (2007; 2009) observes from his clinical practice the phenomenon of overprotective parenting in low-risk environments that characterizes the experience of Western middle-class families today. He notes that overprotective parenting in urban middle-class families is on the rise even though the world is safer for such families today than ever before. He asserts that swelling numbers of smaller, middle-class families, and rising aspirations for children's future success, as well as fears of the world becoming increasingly dangerous are possible factors influencing the emergence of overprotective parenting. Ungar (2009) argues that he has observed in young people two possible consequences of overprotective parenting. First, that they will imbibe and even internalize their parents' worries and thus withdraw from scenarios that present risk, possibly becoming over-anxious about the environment they inhabit. Second, that having been shielded from risk, young people will actively seek out their own ways of experiencing risk beyond the realms of parental oversight, likely with their peers in possibly deleterious ways. One popular term used to describe overprotective parenting is "helicopter parenting." The term first emerged in the US mainstream media in 1991 (Bristow 2014) to refer to parents or guardians who cannot help but hover around the young people under their care, so that they can be extremely prompt in rendering assistance even if it is unsolicited or unwelcome. The corollary to the helicopter parent is of course the "cotton wool kid" who is deemed soft and defenseless, and always in need of adult intervention to survive.

However, rather than attribute blame for overprotective parenting to parents themselves, critics argue that we need to seek the "cultural source of the problem" (Bristow 2014, 201). In other words, what broader societal discourse is raising parental concerns that in turn trigger overprotective parenting practices? Commentators contend that it is the language and logics of risk assessment that have shaped perceptions of parenting and pervaded parenting practices. Lee (2014) articulates the notion of "risk consciousness" (10–11), where people have come to perceive risk not as a probability but as an "untoward possibility" that they seek to avert. Such risk consciousness, when applied to children, frames them as vulnerable to various forms of undesirable possibilities that parents must endeavor to manage or mitigate. To this end, parents should therefore go beyond nurturing and stimulating their children; they need to monitor them to safeguard them from risks. Parents thus have to develop "risk management strategies" (14), especially in light of the advice they are deluged with about various risks and dangers that are inimical to their children's well-being. Lee (2014) notes that risk consciousness seems to have risen since the 1970s and is further amplified by "risk entrepreneurs" (Hunt 2003) who engage in the promotion of particular risks to sell their own expertise and undermine traditional authorities. Risk promotion as pertaining to children can be noted in various issues, including nutrition, cognitive development, socioemotional maturation, online and offline safety, where risk entrepreneurs seek to peddle services that can help overcome or minimize risks in any of those areas.

Ultimately, paranoid parenting and other analogous concepts reflect the important position children can assume in their parents' lives, as well as current societal valorization of children. Viviana Zelizer writes in *Pricing the Priceless Child* (1994) that children today are seen to be economically worthless because they do not make economic contributions to the family as children did in the past. Yet they are "emotionally priceless" and have become objects of affect and sentiment. As Furedi (2008) notes, "emotional investment in children becomes so encompassing that parents' social and moral identities become inseparable from their parenting identities" (118).

PARENTING PRIORITIES IN ASIA

Indeed, parenting concepts relating to intensive or even overparenting, although originating in the United States, have gained traction in many parts of the world including Asia. The situation is especially pronounced in Asia where education is highly valued and is almost universally regarded as the guaranteed path to upward social mobility. To foreground the readers' understanding of parenting in Singapore, I will delve more deeply into parenting priorities in Asia.

Singapore's multiethnic population of Chinese, Malays, Indians, and Eurasians who trace their roots to diverse parts of Asia is the result of past immigration (Winstedt et al. 2019). Its status as a former British colony led to English being adopted by the country's post-independence leaders as the lingua franca, used in business, administration, and education. Despite the population's ostensibly Western outlook, Singaporeans' family values remain influenced by their ethnic cultures and are reflected in their approach to parenting.

Many Asian societies, including Japan, Singapore, and South Korea, subscribe to notions of idealized motherhood wherein the mother is tasked with raising "quality children" (Yeoh and Huang 2010, 48) by dedicating themselves to their children's needs, especially those pertaining to education. In Hong Kong for example, Karsten (2015) observed that intensive parenting involves parents engaging in extensive communication with schools, private tutors, and domestic helpers to closely supervise the children's schoolwork and enrichment activities, to the point that some mothers quit their jobs or shorten their working hours to fully commit to these parenting tasks. Similarly, in Singapore, mothers are expected to serve as the children's "key educational agent" and to practice "discretionary mothering" (Yeoh and Huang 2010, 32), where they pour their energies into higher order responsibilities, such as supervising their children's academic work, while delegating rudimentary caregiving and housekeeping duties to hired help. As well, Göransson (2015) found that parents in Singapore tend to find the education system highly competitive and are driven to devote extensive time, energy, and financial wherewithal to their children's education, for fear of them falling behind their peers.

Even with the diversity in Asia, some common threads can be discerned in terms of the primary duties considered critical for parents to fulfill. Research suggests that these are inculcation of values in children; oversight and supervision of children to protect them from harm and adverse influence; and support of children in their academic achievement. Taken together, these key parental duties are all undertaken with a view toward preparing children to become independent and productive members of society.

The inculcation of values serves as a key parenting priority in most Asian societies. Historical perspectives of childhood in Asia, influenced by both Confucian doctrine and Buddhist philosophy, suggest that children are born good and pure, tainted only by the adult world and their external environment. To shield children from such adverse influences, parents must steer their children onto the right path by educating them and instilling in them the right values.

Chinese parents, for example, view the inculcation of values as a task of "training" the child (Chao 1995; Chen and Luster 2002). They believe that children's personal development is influenced more by the environment than by hereditary factors (Ho and Kang 1984) and see parental nurturance as key to a child's positive growth. Effort is thus prized over inherent ability, and parents must therefore strive to encourage effort and shape a supportive home environment to instill in their children positive values. This raises the question of what parents are actually training the child in. Principally, values such as "impulse control" and self-regulation are considered ideal qualities that children must acquire to be well-functioning individuals. Correspondingly, if parents fail to offer effective "family education" and their children misbehave, parents can be taken to task and criticized for being derelict in their duties (Kelly and Tseng 1992).

In a bid to imbue in their children positive values, Chinese parents tend to adopt more authoritarian and authoritative styles where they control (*guan*) their children fairly strictly. Such "control" does not have draconian connotations but is instead assumed to be born out of love for the child and is ultimately an expression of care (Pomerantz and Wang 2009; Tobin, Wu, and Davidson 1991). By the same token, children in many East Asian cultures may not regard parental control as an infringement of their personal autonomy but take it as a key dimension of the parent-child compact (Lee, Yu, and Choi 2012). Indeed, parents who do not exercise control over their children are deemed negligent and uncaring. Consequently, parents adopt disciplining strategies such as imposing rules and restrictions that are accompanied by reasoning and may even employ mild verbal or physical punishment when the child does not comply (Xu et al. 1991; Lin 1999). Traditional Chinese parenting regards mild corporal punishment as a useful aid for correcting children's misbehavior and instilling discipline. These can include light palm swatting or being made to stand and face a wall.

Asian cultures also regard interdependence as the cornerstone of familial relationships (Chao and Tseng 2005). Children are therefore socialized to regard the family as their main locus in life, and to treasure kinship ties above all else. In this collectivistic mold, individualism and independence are downplayed and group goals are prioritized over personal ones. Confucian societies thus stress interdependence and harmony within the family, and childrearing practices in Asia are accordingly shaped. For instance, a comparison of childrearing practices of immigrant Chinese and European mothers in America found that while both groups stress love for the child, the former sees loving the child as the key to a strong and lasting parent-child relationship, while the latter believes that it is critical to raising the child's self-esteem (Chao 1995). To achieve familial harmony and relational goals, family members perform different roles that are underlined by care, reciprocity, and mutual obligation. Parental authority takes precedence, and children must in turn fulfill obligations and duties to the family (Chao and Tseng 2005). Parents also seek to shield their children from adverse influence from peers and other individuals they interact with.

Parental authority is primarily exercised through oversight and supervision of children, considered a principal responsibility of parents in Asia. In Confucian doctrine, the family's identity is intricately linked to the outcomes of its members (Kibria 1993). Hence, parents are obligated to monitor their children's behavior and their circles of friends to prevent deviant behavior that can undermine the family's social standing (Gorman 1998; Xiong et al. 2005). In her study comprising observations of Hong Kong families, Karsten (2015) found that children are accompanied at all times even though it is considered a safe city, with adults outnumbering children at playgrounds. This instinct to supervise the children closely is thus deeply rooted in the middle-class discourse on good parenthood, where leaving the child alone is frowned upon.

Indeed, Asian parents have been known to consider their protective approach and active involvement in their children's lives as a key contributor to their children's success (Gorman 1998; Chua 2011). While proactive monitoring is a well-established disposition of all parents (Valkenburg and Piotrowski 2017), previous research suggests that overprotective parenting is more common among Asian parents and may even be commonly accepted, stretching even into adolescence and adulthood (Lowinger and Kwok 2001).

Besides merely inculcating values in their children and protecting them from physical harm, supporting their academic pursuits is another key responsibility of parents in Asian societies (Chao and Tseng 2005; Chao 1995). In many Asian cultures, educating a child is analogized to planting a tree that must be diligently cultivated and nurtured. Parents are thus akin to tireless gardeners who must cultivate their children by providing them with all manner of educational and other advantages that can grant them social mobility. Indeed, Confucian philosophies assert that humans can and should be molded in a quest for self-improvement that can be aided with individual effort. In line with such beliefs, Asian parents set lofty educational goals for their children and have high expectations for the grades they should attain and the effort they should expend in pursuit of the same (Hau and Salili 1991; Salili 1996). Children are thus encouraged to study for long periods of time in pursuit of excellent grades (Luo et al. 2013; Salili, Chiu, and Lai 2001).

With this premium placed on academic achievement, parents in many Asian societies are heavily involved in various aspects of their children's schooling. Previous research has identified different forms of parental involvement in the child's schooling, also referred to as parent school involvement (Fan and Chen 2001). These include setting goals and expectations for children's academic achievement; taking part in school activities and programs, such as volunteering; parent-child discussions about school; and creating a home setting conducive for studying (Katz et al. 1993; Chao and Tseng 2005). Another important activity is home-school conferencing, referring to parents' communications with teachers that serve to bridge the gap between home and school, such as communicating with teachers via telephone, e-mail, or attending parent-teacher conferences (Stright and Yeo 2014). Such school-focused parenting practices have been found to influence children's academic performance because they can affect children's motivation, offer them a sense of security, and even help children value education (Gonzalez-DeHass, Willems, and Holbein 2005). Furthermore, school-focused parenting practices give parents a closer understanding of subject content their children are engaging with, homework, and their children's conduct in school, thereby helping them better support their children's educational pursuits and academic conduct (Hill and Taylor 2004). Notably, parent school involvement has been found to be beneficial especially for less educated parents, with stronger relationships found between parent school involvement and children's achievement for such parents (Domina 2005).

Other forms of parental support that are not directly related to school but nevertheless help the child academically have also been identified, including providing children with opportunities for practice and a positive, edifying home environment (Epstein 1995). In this regard, activities such as taking the child to watch plays and concerts, exposing them to venues such as museums and libraries, and reading to them would also be considered activities that constitute positive parental academic support.

In Singapore for example, Clarke (2001) provides a vivid account of how parents are expected to play an active, multifaceted role in the child's education. Her study was geared toward providing guidance on how schools can better prepare parents for their roles in their children's educational journey. She found that quite apart from ensuring that the child attends school regularly, parents are encouraged to volunteer at school through fundraising or other supporting activities. Outside of school hours, parents must also supervise homework and manage school-home communication on general reminders as well as those regarding their child's academic progress. Beyond the child's immediate school environment, many parents also assume additional duties such as taking the child to and from private tuition and enrichment classes, and even attending relevant parenting workshops and talks to better inform themselves.

Parents in Singapore also invest heavily in private tutoring and enrichment classes in a bid to help their children outperform their peers (Barr and Skrbiš 2008). Indeed, this practice has even been referred to as an "educational arms race" (Gee 2012) that is perpetuated by the "parentocracy"—where educational outcomes are determined more by parents' aspirations and socioeconomic capital than by children's innate abilities (Tan 2017). The situation in Hong Kong is very similar. Here too, they hold their children to high standards academically, although there have been arguments that the exclusive emphasis on academic achievement of parents of working-class and poor families in Hong Kong may not ensure upward mobility for their children (Choi 2016). These parents intensively enroll their preschoolers in two kindergartens a day (Choi 2016) and their older children in enrichment classes that can help build their personal portfolio to ensure acceptance into highly selective schools, from even elementary school age. So pervasive are private tuition classes in Asia that they have been termed the "shadow education industry" (Bray and Lykins 2012), an increasingly lucrative sector offering after-school tuition classes that promise to bolster children's academic achievements (Wise 2016). Such classes are geared toward shaping high performers and involve additional hours of classroom instruction and homework, thereby inflating the amount of time children spend on academic work. Quite apart from the high costs of such classes, they impose additional stress on children and a growing parental burden to fund and coordinate their children's increasingly intense academic schedule.

This belief in the importance of after-school academic reinforcement is increasingly accompanied by an interest to develop children's excellence in extra-curricular areas such as sports and the arts. "Enrichment classes" lessons in swimming, taekwondo, soccer, ballet, piano, violin, and visual arts are widely offered and in great demand throughout cities in Asia. Parents believe that exposure to such activities can aid in their children's personal development, while also lending them an edge when applying to sought-after schools. Ultimately, such parental investment is a positional good (Frank 1985) that raises the competition among parents (and children) to outdo one another in the race for academic and extra-curricular excellence.

Essentially all these efforts translate into highly scheduled lives for both parents and children and greater expectations for children to perform well in multiple realms. In sum, the burden on parents in many urbanized Asian societies to plan and micro-coordinate their lives around their children's busy schedules and diverse obligations is hefty.

TECHNOLOGY IN PARENTING

Indeed, the daily hubbub of family life involves getting in sync the needs and priorities of different family members, so that obligations both within and beyond the home are fulfilled, with parents seeking to iron out any kinks with the best coordination they can muster. The entry of accessible and affordable mobile communication technologies that helped make such coordination more seamless led to the growing deployment of mobile media in the performance of parenting. In a pioneering study, Rakow and Navarro (1993) delved into women's use of cellular phones in cars to understand how they incorporated mobile media into their lives. They found that women actively used these car phones for the micro-coordination of family schedules and general household management, and they were prescient in identifying the phenomenon of "remote mothering." Rakow and Navarro's work also struck an early note of ambivalence, arguing that the inextricable link to home life was as burdensome as it was beneficial. The women they interviewed were less than enthused about owning a mobile phone and saw it as more of an instrumental tool for enhancing their personal safety and their availability to their children.

As mobile phone adoption grew, their use in family micro-coordination became more prevalent, especially when it was not only parents but also children who started to own mobile phones. A study by Ling and Yttri (2002) on the situation in Norway found that dual-career parents used the mobile phone's calling and texting functions for coordinating mundane but nonetheless essential everyday activities. Dynamic arrangements around grocery shopping or driving children to and from lessons were made on the fly, while family members were in transit. Since those early days, the deployment of mobile media for micro-coordination has become more fervent with significant strides in smartphone technology and mobile media adoption. As Lynn Schofield Clark noted in *The Parent App* (2013), smartphones and their slew of apps are increasingly critical in helping parents coordinate the family's daily whirr of activities, and yet these apparent aids are another imposition on parents, necessitating the constant updating and synchronization of schedules among all family members.

Aside from micro-coordination, parents instinctively and increasingly leveraged their newfound connections with their children to monitor and enhance their well-being. Ling and Yttri (2002) found that the mobile phone was also used as a safeguard to keep tabs on their children's whereabouts and to contact them in case of exigencies or emergencies. Indeed, risk perceptions tend to encourage parents to equip children with mobile phones. Matsuda's (2008) investigation into mothers of elementary school children in Japan revealed that concerns about children's safety elide with notions of maternal responsibility, thus engendering a climate where parents feel obliged to give their children mobile phones, even at very tender ages. Indeed, the parental instinct to check on their children's safety and welfare does not seem to wane as the children grow older. My study of middle-class mothers in China and South Korea found that they appreciated being constantly connected to their children, although they were at times unnerved by how this ceaseless connectivity meant that they had to constantly "keep watch" over their children (Lim and Soon 2010). These findings were echoed in our research on left-behind parents in Vietnam whose children were studying at universities in Singapore. These parents insisted that their university-aged children in Singapore should always pick up calls from them, failing which they would scrutinize the child's social media feeds to assess their recent activity. Parents would also actively contact their children's friends in Singapore just to reassure themselves, and, often, such parental anxiety turned out to be misplaced (Pham and Lim 2018). Hence, as mobile media extend their reach and link networks of people in unprecedented ways, the use of technology in parenting continues to assume fresh forms of parental intervention.

Micro-coordination and connectivity between parents and children aside, the frequency, duration, and nature of such technology-enabled communication can have an influence on family relationships. Studying parents and teenagers in Israel, Ribak (2009) argued that the mobile phone served as a pivotal vehicle for intergenerational communication, a de facto "remote control" for parental supervision.

She also likened the mobile phone to an "umbilical cord" that intimately and discreetly connected parents and teenagers and would ultimately dry up and fall off with healthy separation. For these Israeli parents and teenagers, the mobile phone at first brush seemed to offer prosaic connectivity involving mainly the exchange of short transactional messages. However, closer exploration revealed that the mobile phone played the lofty role of reassuring these parents that they could easily contact their children should the need arise. And yet, more communication does not necessarily guarantee stronger bonds. Weisskirch (2009) surveyed mobile phone use by American parents and adolescents. Parents who called their adolescents more often or when upset tended to experience greater familial disharmony, while children who called their parents for social support reported greater parental knowledge and better relationships.

Naturally, the parenting remit is sizeable and goes far beyond coordinating schedules, ensuring safety, and maintaining relationships. Technology is indeed also an invaluable resource for parents in terms of the information they need and the opportunities they seek. A large body of research has thus focused on how parents, especially mothers rather than fathers, appropriate various technology platforms to solicit support and exchange parenting experiences to cope with the tribulations of parenthood. Since the 1990s, mothers have found solace and solidarity on parenting websites and online discussion forums, to, more recently, parenting blogs and social media, although such online sources complement rather than supersede the advice of healthcare professionals or trusted family members (Lupton, Pedersen, and Thomas 2016). Katz and Gonzalez (2016) found that low-income Latino families in the United States welcomed technologies such as computers and the Internet into their home and household matters. These parents actively made use of online resources and translation tools to find out about and help with their children's homework or to look up medical information on websites, such as WebMD, when their children were sick. Similarly, Wilson and Yochim's (2017) study of working- and middle-class stay-at-home mothers in the United States found that these women draw heavily upon online resources such as parenting websites and "mommy blogs" and online communities on Facebook, Instagram, and Pinterest for material and emotional support. For example, some would engage in "couponing" while in the car waiting for their children, obtaining discounts for necessities to help the family economize. A more recent trend in the use of technology in parenting pertains specifically to pregnant mothers. Emerging research from the past five years has seen the explosion of pregnancy apps that can be connected to wearable devices to facilitate the tracking of conception, fetal growth, heart rate, movements, and biometrics, including even the taking and sharing photographs of baby bumps (Godwin 2019). Indeed, market research has shown that pregnancy-app downloads are more popular than fitness-app downloads (Lupton, Pedersen, and Thomas 2016). Leaver (2017) argued that as more data for and about babies become readily available, parental tracking and monitoring via such pregnancy apps and smart devices are being normalized as a necessary component of parental care. In such a metrics-driven parenting culture, failure to adopt and exploit such apps in the child's interest could be deemed a dereliction of parental duty.

The progressively rising tempo in the use of mobile media to perform parenting duties has thus culminated in the situation we see today in many urban societies. Mobile media have become an indispensable and indeed gargantuan part of the parenting toolkit, constituting the virtual nerve center of family operations. Above and beyond parents electing to use mobile media to smooth their daily communication and coordination, the institutions surrounding themselves and their children, namely workplaces, childcare centers, and schools, are also avidly using mobile media in the provision of their services, thereby reshaping parenting practices through a myriad of digital affordances and transformations. Livingstone and Blum-Ross (2018) asked British parents to identify their perceived changes in the media landscape through comparing their own childhoods with their children's more digitalized ones. These parents saw this generational change as "different," "unrecognizable," or even "intense" and expressed hopes that their children would acquire the competencies to keep up with a fast-moving digital future riddled with unreliable and precarious technologies.

Mobile media have thus increasingly become a convenient, but intensive, datafied channel through which parents learn about parenting, discuss parenting practices and set parenting norms, manage their identities as parents, perform "ideal" parenthood, and express intimacy for themselves, their families, and social networks (Lupton, Pedersen, and Thomas 2016). Parents now have to negotiate their perceptions, practices, and priorities along a challenging path—from their minimally or non-digitalized past to their children's media-laden present—toward an uncertain digital future filled with possibilities and risks (Livingstone and Blum-Ross 2018). These individual and societal shifts have served to entrench mobile media in family life, thereby paving the way for transcendent parenting.

Indeed, as I explained in Chapter 1, I do not conceive of transcendent parenting as a form of parenting in and of itself, but as a parenting practice that has emerged from a technologically infused environment marked by the intensifying use of mobile media in both the broader societal landscape and in the home. Hence, transcendent parenting must be further understood within the context of parenting practices writ large, as well as the parenting priorities that are salient among the urban middle class. In the upcoming chapters, I will delve into the different parenting responsibilities that align with these parenting goals and present evidence from my research on Singapore families to show how transcendent parenting has manifested itself in today's mobile media-infused landscape.

3

At Home

At a bench outside an enrichment class center in a mall on a Sunday:

> *Mother: While we wait for your sister's class to end, why don't you learn your spelling?*
>
> *Son: (whining) Must I??? Okay, okay, where is it?*
>
> *Mother: Aiyah! I saved it onto the iPad, but the battery was low, so I left it at home to charge!*
>
> *Father: Isn't the iPad synced to your phone?*
>
> *Mother: No, I didn't save it as an image. It's a PDF and those aren't synced.*
>
> *Father: Why didn't you just save it onto your Dropbox so that you can access it everywhere? Aiyah!*
>
> *Mother: Aiyah! Why is it always my fault? Ryan, after lunch you'd better learn your spelling super-fast before your badminton class later, okay? You'd better not waste time and dilly dally, alright?*
>
> *Son: (grinning and bouncing with glee) Ah, okay, okay . . . Yay! I can rest now.*

I witnessed the scene above while I was waiting for my daughter to finish her art lesson. Every weekend such scenes replay themselves in

Transcendent Parenting. Sun Sun Lim, Oxford University Press (2020).

DOI: 10.1093/oso/9780190088989.001.0001

malls throughout Singapore, of parents hurriedly shepherding their children to and from enrichment classes. While the children are in class, parents wait patiently on benches or in eateries nearby, albeit with an air of resignation. They pass the time by reading newspapers or chatting with other parents. Most busy themselves on their phones, reading and sending WhatsApp messages, scrolling through their Facebook feeds, or matching the jelly beans on Candy Crush. Younger siblings who grow restless with the wait are indulged with videos or games on their own tablet devices. Now and then, I overhear conversations like the one above that constantly remind me of how involved parents in Singapore are in their children's education and what a significant role mobile devices have come to play in their family life. I also hear various phone calls made: parents instructing domestic helpers on chores to be completed; mothers asking fathers to pick up their kids; fathers reminding their children to wait punctually at the schoolgate to avoid traffic delays during pickups, and so on. These are families whose lives are lubricated by mobile connections, the absence of which would spell inconvenience, frustration, inefficiency, drudgery, and perhaps even helplessness. And yet the presence and salience of mobile connections in the chug of their everyday lives also introduces friction, stress, and pressure that complicate parental responsibilities, setting the stage for transcendent parenting.

The key to grasping the context that the transcendent parent inhabits is to first understand parents' sense of their role as nurturers of their children. As Furedi (2002) observes, the trope of parental determinism has strengthened over time, and societal perceptions that parental influence is fundamental to a child's development is increasingly unquestioned. Indeed, my respondents seemed to buy wholeheartedly into this notion and took seriously their multifaceted responsibilities toward their children—as caregiver, disciplinarian, teacher, friend, counsellor, advocate, and even manager. They identified and explicated each of these roles, as they shared their hopes and aspirations for their children, strategies they had developed to guide them, challenges they encountered in parenting, and the solutions they developed in response. In the context of these experiences, they also delved into those pertaining to the use of mobile media in their homes, how they mediated their children's technology use, and the varied ways in which mobile communication shaped their family practices, habits, and routines, for good or for ill.

PARENTAL ASPIRATIONS

As I discussed in the previous chapter, among the urban middle class in Asia, great premium is placed on academic achievement, and all these efforts are geared toward raising their children's chances of academic success (Chao and Tseng 2005; Yeoh and Huang 2010). When our respondents shared their hopes for their children, the discussions would often begin with parents reflecting on the importance of academic excellence, as exemplified by the following quotes (to protect their privacy, the names of all interviewees quoted throughout the book are pseudonyms):

> *Though I know that the totality is not just about results but also about the well-being of the kid, we still want them to secure a job. In order for you to get into a university, you need that paper qualification first, even when you don't really utilize it when you go to work, as work actually has more to do with experience. It's just like a passport to enter whatever you want. So I still need to emphasize that [my son] needs to score in order for him to excel. But of course I won't set the expectation like he needs to be the best among the best.—Abigail Liu, mother of one son aged 8*
>
> *But studies are still important. I mean the living cost in Singapore is quite high, you need the paper qualifications to get better jobs. My*

> *husband and I, we didn't have good qualifications. I mean, now that he's self-employed, we can maintain the household, but it's a rather manual labor job. I think with better paper qualifications it helps in many ways. Maybe four to five years ago, a polytechnic diploma is sufficient. But I think now the basic [requirement] is you have to go to polytechnic, then university. If my kids pay attention in class, do their revision at home, I think they can do it. Performing slightly above average will do. You don't have to compete with people with very good background and very good qualifications.—Judy Lau, mother of two children aged 11 and 14*

These views echo those of most respondents and accord with research that has found that, in many Asian societies, academic qualifications are considered integral to a person's ability to succeed in life and also to attain social mobility, security, and comfort (see for example Clark, Mountford-Zimdars, and Francis 2015; Saw, Berenbaum, and Okazaki 2013). Clearly, Judy wished for her children to perform well academically to exceed her and her husband, neither of whom had attained the academic qualifications that she deems indispensable to a bright future.

At the same time though, she perceived that the demands for academic qualifications had become more onerous over time, where nothing less than a university degree is required to pursue attractive employment opportunities. Yet, not wishing to impose undue pressure on her children, her ambition was tempered with reason. Notably, she recognized that her children do not have to strive to be the crème de la crème as they did not enjoy the natural trappings of socioeconomic privilege. Hence, she rationalized that as long as they put in effort, they should be able to perform slightly better than their peers, and that this approach should set them on the right path.

Other parents, however, could be quite explicitly performance oriented. In the case of the next parent you will hear from, she felt that since her older son had been identified to be academically gifted, he was capable of attaining outstanding results and her task as a parent was to motivate him to do better by setting goals that would stretch his abilities:

> *I just want my sons to be healthy, happy. For the elder boy, I would expect higher [performance] since he entered the GEP [Gifted Education Program]. We were really hands on. His father would help him, assist him, force him to do filing, checking, homework. We would ask him, "Have you done this this and that?" We just wanted him to reach certain expectations. They have certain scores you must get. He always just touches the line. Yes, it's a problem. Even now, he is still like that. He has to work under stress. You stress him, he can go through more. But (sigh), it's unhealthy . . . He definitely can do better! So we must set standards for him, "You must get certain marks!"—Violet Cheung, mother of two sons aged 9 and 15*

Indeed, it has been firmly established that grade orientation is especially salient among families in Asian countries (Hau and Salili 1991; Salili 1996). The valorization of good grades is well illustrated by Figure 3.1, a group chat to which I personally belonged, comprising parents of my son's primary 6 classmates. In Singapore, all primary 6 students attending national schools must, at the age of 12, take the Primary School Leaving Examination (PSLE). This examination is considered "high stakes" because it determines which secondary school the child can qualify for, and the child's grades can mean the difference between entering a better "elite school" or a more mediocre "neighborhood school." It is in precisely such a high-stakes context that the "shadow education industry" is booming in places such as Singapore, Hong Kong, and South Korea (Barr and Skrbiš 2008; Bray and Lykins 2012; Gee 2012).

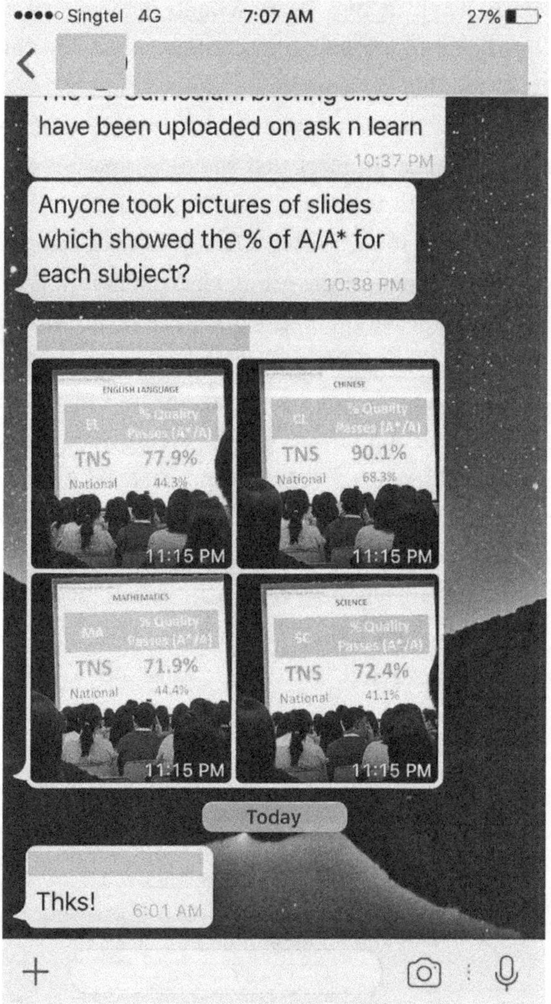

Figure 3.1 WhatsApp parents' chat group sharing photographs of a school briefing where information on the school's performance for the previous year's Primary School Leaving Examination was announced.

Notably, as is typical of primary schools in Singapore, my son's school had organized a briefing session for parents on this major examination, and one key component covered was the percentage of "quality passes," that is, A* and A, that the previous cohort of students had attained. The fact that such information was shared at the briefing—and at the very start of the academic year—amply reflects the concern about grades. On top of that, the screenshot also shows that a parent in the group chat inquired if anyone had taken down the information on the grades attained, while another parent promptly posted all the relevant photographs he had taken. This interest in grades is not surprising and can be noted in online parenting discussion forums where parents share the scores of top students in different schools, and private enrichment centers circulate flyers that indicate the scores of their top performing students as well. Indeed, as you can see in Figure 3.2, some enrichment centers are known to offer their own awards for their top performing students to signal their commitment (and ability) to help their students perform well.

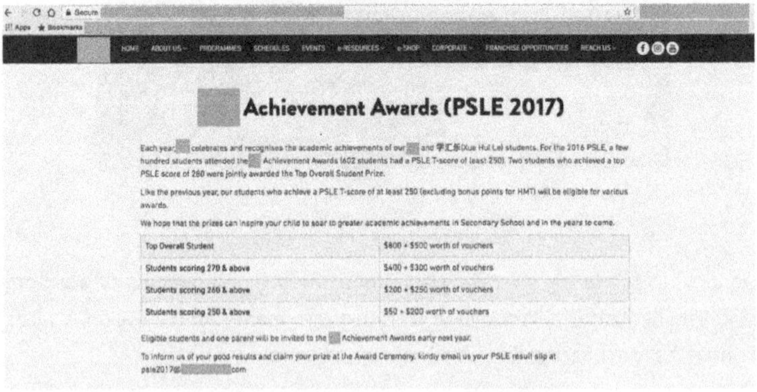

Figure 3.2 Screenshot of enrichment center's website information about special awards for top students.

Unsurprisingly, given this concern among Singapore parents for children to excel academically, our respondents admitted to a very high level of parental involvement in their children's school-related matters.

> *I always make the time to attend the school's parent-teacher meetings. That's my priority. Not often, but sometimes we have to take leave from work, you know. If I really cannot make it, then my husband has to. I will be the one to attend, unless I really cannot. We want to find out how the child is doing, how we can help them improve.—Yvette Lim, full-time working mother of two daughters aged 9 and 13*

As Yvette's view manifests, there is a strong sense of parental commitment to school activities that have a direct bearing on the child's academic performance, such that parents will make a concerted effort to carve out time from their packed schedules. Indeed, her behavior is very consistent with the concerted cultivation observed by Lareau (2003) of middle-class parents in the United States. This quote also reflects the strong expectation that Singapore parents be deeply involved in their children's academic endeavors, from providing support at home to being active in the child's school as well (Clarke 2001). Notably too, Yvette speaks with a palpable sense of purpose about making sure she knows how her child is faring to help her do better in school.

PARENTAL RESPONSIBILITIES

Hence, these parents' diligent and vigilant supervision of their children's academic performance is very much a reflection of their parental and familial aspirations. All the way from preschool through to adolescence, our respondents were, without exception, invested in providing the best home for their children, materially, socially, and emotionally. Parents would share the spectrum of tasks they felt constituted their key parenting responsibilities. As one respondent itemized:

> *Number one thing, feeding them physically so that they can keep up with their academic learning and emotional development. Number two, keeping up with the important dates in their life, so there's a lot of important dates in a child's calendar, which includes exams, competitions, enrichment, or whatsoever, and sometimes things can get pretty messed up, or things can overlap. Then number three is supporting them and their questions, be their tuition teacher.—Esther Lee, mother of three children aged 5, 11, and 13*

Esther's view exemplifies the parental determinism (Faircloth 2014; Furedi 2002) that pervades current thinking about parenting and the growing notion that parents must strive to be the foremost authorities on all aspects of their children's development (Wolf 2010). It is also telling that the parenting responsibilities she articulates are all directly or indirectly oriented toward boosting her children's academic potential, pointing again to the valorization of academic excellence.

For families with preschool children, parents put considerable effort into ensuring that their children had access to a vast range of diversions to stimulate them intellectually and to boost their sociocognitive development. As Katz (2008) has observed, childhood has become the prime arena where parents engage in material acquisition and social practices to give their children a leg up over their peers. Indeed, the typical preschooler's home was usually well equipped with child-friendly toys and books, often located in a dedicated area of the home specifically set aside for the child to independently and freely play, such as the typical preschooler's "play and learning corner" in a Singaporean household captured in Figure 3.3. Parents would also explain how particular toys and books had been

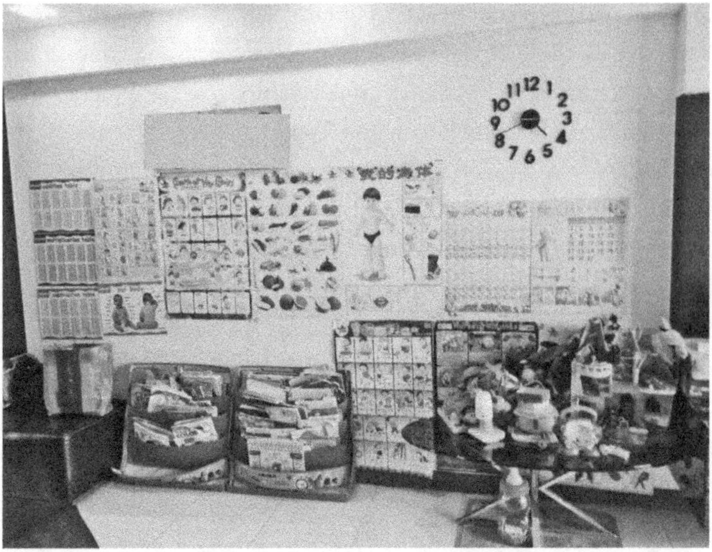

Figure 3.3 A typical preschooler's "play and learning corner" set up at home by the parents.

purchased for their educational value, strategically placed in shelves or containers for the children to access with minimal adult assistance.

This zeal to create a safe and nourishing physical environment was extended to the virtual spaces that the children could enter, primarily via tablet devices. This was something the parents of preschoolers paid special attention to since their children were too young to make independent choices in this regard. These parents curated the devices with apps that they felt were age appropriate and would fully stimulate their children's sociocognitive development.

With the strong societal emphasis on children's academic performance, among the families with children in primary and secondary schools, there was a strong orientation toward shaping the home environment in a way that the child could thrive academically, again a reflection of concerted cultivation (Lareau 2003). As previous research on Asian parents has shown, they assiduously ensure that their children have all the material trappings that confer strong educational benefit such as books, dictionaries, calculators, and computers, often with significant benefits (Chao and Tseng 2005). Our respondents were similarly conscientious, making sure their children were well provided for in this respect.

Beyond catering to these material needs and wants, another key component of a hospitable home environment for education is parental involvement in the child's schooling. An extensive body of research concurs that when families are more involved in their children's education, children attain better grades, attend school more consistently, are more socially adept, present fewer disciplinary issues, and advance to higher levels of academic achievement (Chaboudy and Jameson 2001; Fan and Chen 2001; Henderson and Mapp 2002). Indeed, our respondents with children in primary and secondary schools also had to tirelessly manage the busy schedules of their children, resonating with the findings of research that Singapore parents expend considerable time, energy, and financial resources to play an active role in children's education (Clarke 2001; Göransson 2015). Most respondents noted that school hours were long because after the official school day was over, children would have co-curricular activities, and some would also attend extra tuition classes with private tutors or at private tuition centers to supplement their formal schooling. Of course, children would also have homework to complete, often daily, thus leaving them with relatively little unstructured or leisure time on school days. As Lisa Lin, a 39-year-old working mother to a 12-year-old girl in secondary school and a 10-year-old boy in primary school recounted:

> *Both [my children] have quite tight schedules. They reach home at about four plus. My mom is at home helping me. After office hours*

> *when we reach home, [my husband and I] will check both of their schoolbags, to find out whether they forget to do any homework. From primary one I already did that so they are used to me checking their schoolbags and helping them pack. Their homework is a lot, so I don't mind helping them pack the next day's schoolbag, even for my Sec[ondary] One girl, although I know I am supposed to let her do it alone. Monday and Tuesday she will reach home maybe even later than me, because of the co-curricular activities. By the time she reaches home, it's seven thirty. After dinner, she still needs to do homework. What can I do? I just help them out to ease a bit of work. If I don't help them, they will have to check and pack their bags, so may as well use this time to let them do their school homework. My husband is more like a behind the scenes helper. He lets me do everything first until I cannot cope. I don't have much time to talk to them, only at weekends. So when I pack their schoolbags [on weekdays], I will ask them, "Today what is the school homework? Have you taken care of everything? How is your school day?" These are the routine questions that I keep asking.*

As Lisa's account reveals, the daily routine of the Singaporean family with school-going children centers tightly on academic pursuits with parents being highly involved. Homework is the foremost priority, and the hectic schedules of both parents and children demand efficient, effective, and disciplined time management. Indeed, it appears that a great deal of parental labor is dedicated to ensuring that the children's schooling responsibilities are duly fulfilled, both in terms of completing homework and being prepared for the next school day, harking to the "parenting time famine" that Furedi (2002, 90) has pronounced. On such schooldays, task-oriented communication tends to dominate as parents and children work together as a well-oiled unit to tackle all these academic obligations.

> *After I started to use ClassDojo, I am more involved as a working mom. Working moms always have this guilty feeling because we don't have more time for the child. For myself, I have to work late. By the time I reach home, she may already be asleep. But throughout the day, I can check the app anytime. If I know there's homework, I will share with my husband, "Just take note, because I will be late, I won't be home early." Maybe he can help to guide [my daughter]. I can share my burden. Sometimes I am scared that I forget, I will WhatsApp him because there are so many things. Last time, without all these apps, I had to call [the school's office], then they said I would have to e-mail. It was a struggle! You had to call, then you were busy with your work, meetings all that. By the time you remembered [that you had to call again], the teacher might already have left the school."—Yvette Lim, 37, full-time working mother of two children aged 9 and 13*

As Yvette's sharing shows, parents possess a very strong sense of duty with regard to overseeing their children's studies, even as they have to manage their own professional obligations. Hence, Yvette regarded the ClassDojo app as a veritable boon that helped her to be more involved in her younger child's studies and to be especially vigilant about ensuring that homework is duly completed. By keeping herself well-informed during the workday, Yvette could also assuage her guilt as a working mother who felt she had less time to spend with her children. Her struggle to juggle parenting and professional duties echoes the observations made by Lana Rakow and Vija Navarro (1993) who noted the "parallel shift" that women perform when their cellular phones increased their availability to their children while they were at work. Indeed, her views encapsulate concerns that parents increasingly labor under "cultural scripts" and normative parenting standards to which they must conform for the benefit of their children (Faircloth 2014).

To this end, some parents would make an extra effort to utilize apps they had downloaded to actively oversee their children's homework.

> *It's called "My Homework." My son can create all the different subjects [in the app]. Most importantly, I want to know what homework is being given to them. They will key in the homework and the deadline. It's their [my children's] responsibility [to key it in]. They have the most updated information from the teacher. The moment they key it in, when I turn on the app at home, straightaway I can see my son's got this homework deadline. It's a form of a journal for them to keep, so they won't miss homework deadlines. It can sync between devices if you log in to the same account. I can help him to keep track of what's going on also.—David Cheung, father of two sons aged 9 and 15*

As David's quote reveals, the children's school obligations are actively factored into the parents' schedules, and families use mobile communication devices and services to keep a handle on things. Such behavior is analogous to the hypervigilance that Nelson (2010) had noted in American parents who actively use technological aids such as baby monitors and mobile phones to keep tabs on their children's well-being. Notably too, these apps enable and encourage a high level of direct parental involvement in their children's education as I will elaborate in Chapter 4.

Therefore, parents do seem to be on a permanent night shift of parenting duties, where, after returning home from work, they must inspect their children's homework and communicate with other parents over WhatsApp to double-check that they (and their children) are completely on top of things:

> *For the elder one, usually we will ask him if he has any homework for that day. Usually he will do it by himself because he is quite afraid*

> *of the teacher. But sometimes he tends to be forgetful and misses certain things. So at the last minute, like that day, eleven p.m., I saw a message on the WhatsApp parents' group, "Oh there's this homework." Maths worksheet or something, then I didn't remember him doing that and he was already in bed, so I just left it. He had to deal with it in school the next day and let the teacher know that he had forgotten to do it. Sometimes the parents' responses [on WhatsApp] are quite late because most of them work late as well, or some of his classmates are in student care and they reach home at seven or seven thirty p.m., then they have dinner, bathe, and start to do homework. So the parents check their kids' schoolbags maybe after eight p.m., then I receive the [WhatsApp] messages when it's already quite late, and we discuss [the children's schoolwork].—Jenna Chang, mother of two children aged 6 and 9*

As Jenna's account indicates, parental involvement can include more mundane tasks such as inspecting and packing their children's schoolbags. Other rudimentary chores include signing permission slips, preparing payment for special activities, and checking with other parents on teachers' reminders. Parents also take upon themselves more laborious duties such as volunteering at school, helping their children complete their homework, and even attending workshops that help parents acquire study strategies and examination tips for their children.

Parents also regard the child's school life as a long-term undertaking and view seriously their role to properly prepare their children for what is effectively their "academic career." Our respondents were wont to speak about their role in guiding their children's academic performance in task-oriented ways, almost akin to a job:

> *First thing I do when I reach home is I check his schoolbag. Every day. I want to set the routine to prepare the child for primary school.*

It has been two months [since he entered primary school]. The transition from preschool hasn't been this easy. [After he reaches home], he will get some of the work done, then play, then we put him to bed. In some sense, yes, I coach my son for his homework. I tell him to take out everything that he needs, then ask him what happened in school today. He has to articulate it. His handwriting is terribly messy. We are still trying to correct him. I would say [my involvement in my son's schoolwork] could be better. [But] we are working parents. We have tried our best.—Amanda Tan, full-time working mother of two sons aged 4 and 7

Amanda speaks as many parents in Singapore do, about commencing primary school as a critical life stage for children, and how she must therefore prepare her child for a smooth transition, illustrating the view that childhood is a crucial period of "accumulation" (Katz 2008). She also refers to how she has to "coach" him to ensure that he can perform critical tasks such as recounting his school day, articulating his homework, and writing legibly, all of which she deems critical for his academic success.

Furthermore, with schools incorporating more digital-learning platforms into their teaching, teachers often explicitly indicated their desire for parental support. As I previously mentioned, parents in Singapore tend to feel a very strong sense of duty in terms of directly supporting their children's learning. For many respondents therefore, especially those with preschool and primary schoolchildren, the teachers requested that parents utilize these platforms at home to extend the child's classroom learning to the domestic realm. For example, some preschools use apps such as Seesaw so their students can practice reading.

Seesaw is more for reading aloud. We will record [the child's reading], then the teacher will review and listen. This is extra [work], yes.

> *I think this is good because now everyone is going towards more IT stuff, so we have to follow the trends as well. I have to use another iPad to have something for him to read from, then I use my phone to record. Once I record, I send it in, then the teacher can assess. This is good. One thing is that I feel that the apps are troublesome but also useful. I can record him, then I play back and see whether he can read correctly. At the beginning, we had to figure our way around the app to make sure that we know how to use the app! I am not that tech-savvy, not ten upon ten, more six to seven, so it takes me more time.—Abigail Liu, mother of one son aged 8*

Our respondents did not find digital-learning platforms entirely intuitive and straightforward, and the amount of effort and time parents had to invest in learning them was certainly not trivial. Such issues led to parents feeling equivocal about such technologies. Indeed, some respondents expressed frustration that schools would employ digital-learning platforms that even older children may not be fully prepared for, whereupon the parents had to step in to offer much-needed assistance:

> *The school recommends Google Classroom. Basically teachers of different subjects will post the homework there. What I do not like is I think sometimes it takes more time to do homework via Google Classroom. Now my daughter has a Chinese project that is graded. So instead of just finding information from the web and writing it out [on paper], you have to type, then download pictures [in Google Classroom]. I think this is a task older kids can do better. My daughter is so little, so I have to help her a bit with how to do it. It's a bit complicated for her, although the teacher did brief them.—Judy Lau, mother of two children aged 11 and 14*

Accounts such as these reflect the broader trend toward homework in schools becoming more complex, to the point that parental involvement is not a luxury but a necessity (Teo 2018). Besides simply requiring academic competencies on the part of the child, such online homework demands technological skills that children have yet to acquire, especially if their parents have actively sought to minimize their screen time, thus limiting their online learning opportunities. Both the mother and father in this family strongly critiqued the extra pressure that the school had put on them and their son through its use of an online assessment tool:

> *During school holidays, there is also assessment online. So we went to ask the teachers, "Is it necessary and compulsory to do it online?" Then they said, "Yes it's compulsory," Then I said, "It will be necessary that the school teaches my son to use a computer, because he is not exposed [to such technologies]." I had to familiarize him with how to use a mouse, because especially when they use a lot of Flash, it's very interactive, so you need a certain amount of maneuvering. I always sit behind him. Sometimes it is tiring for us, because we do not have school holidays. During school holidays, we still have work and still have to monitor the online homework.—Jennifer Tse, mother of three boys aged 1, 5, and 7*

The incorporation of these mobile- or digital-learning platforms is therefore another responsibility that parents must shoulder. The challenges that these parents experienced also raise troubling concerns about inequalities in access and competencies. Specifically, how does the incorporation of these mobile- or digital-learning platforms create disparities in academic performance among children of different socioeconomic classes?

CREATING A HEALTHY MEDIA ENVIRONMENT

One key responsibility of parents, going beyond those related to their children's academic work, is creating a healthy media environment for their children, especially with the proliferation of mobile media devices. Our respondents were deeply sensitive to the highly mediatized society we live in today and expressed a keen interest in overseeing their children's media use. To a greater or lesser extent, all of them felt duty bound to guide their children's media use in light of the deluge of media content they were bombarded with and to curate a media environment that they considered healthy, wholesome, and edifying for the child.

Among parents of preschoolers, many undertook a wide range of efforts to cultivate a positive media milieu for their young children. They would keep a lookout for apps that were age appropriate and had educational value, noting tips from other parents or advice columns they came across in magazines and parenting blogs. One could regard this as a form of intensive parenting (Hays 1996) behavior that is highly child centered, expert guided, emotionally absorbing, and resource intensive. Some would make a special effort to personally try out the apps before they felt comfortable letting their children play with them on their own. Once devices were introduced into the home, parents of preschoolers would introduce rules to maintain what they deemed an optimal level of use. These include limits on the types of content the child could access, such as restricting the number of apps the child could have on the device. Almost all families did not take tablets out of the home because the parents wanted to reduce screen time or found them too heavy to tote along.

Many parents would also impose curbs on when, where, and how long the child could use the tablet and would seek to ensure that secondary caregivers such as domestic helpers or grandparents abide by them. A number of respondents acknowledged that their preschool children would throw tantrums when asked to discontinue using the tablets. Hence some parents would deliberately reduce usage by hiding the device on occasion, keeping it charged to a very low level of battery life so that the device could not be used for too long, or simply lying to the child that the device required charging. Some parents shared how they had encountered problems with their preschool children's device use and efforts they took to resolve them:

> *There was actually a bad experience [with my daughter's device use]. When she was younger, in order to take care of her in a more convenient way, I would show her some videos so I could do some housework. But in the end I didn't expect her to be addicted. Every time she returned from school, the first thing she would ask for was the iPad which I was quite fearful of. In the end I sought help from friends and asked her teachers as well. I found out that she likes crafts, so I let her do some crafts and hands-on activity books. She also developed a hobby for collecting stickers. It distracted her and managed to "chop off" the addiction. We are now maintaining it well and give her ample time to let her know that we will be keeping [the iPad] in how many minutes.—Cheryl Wang, mother of four children aged 1, 3, 14, 16*

For families with children in primary school and beyond, schedules were more hectic and device use at home was more constrained because free time at home was dominated by homework, especially on weekdays. In terms of giving children their personal mobile devices, the most common device was of course the phone, with children in secondary school being given personal laptops if their schools required it. Once children entered upper primary school around the age of 11 or 12, parents were more inclined to give their children personal smartphones, although it was at age 13 when children entered secondary school that most respondents did so. At the time of the research, 2G mobile service had been discontinued in Singapore so feature phones could no longer be used and smartphones were the default option. What usually motivated parents to give their children personal phones was when they started commuting to school on their own and parents wanted the reassurance of contacting them. Alternatively, if the children had many after-school activities, parents wished to be kept updated on their whereabouts. To prevent their children from excessive Internet use on their smartphones therefore, parents tended to load them with prepaid plans that either had no mobile data or very limited access to prevent the children from accessing the Internet.

> *I have this plan with SingTel. Their phone numbers are all tagged with me, so I can control their usage. I can set how much data I want to give them here. I can also switch it off so they don't even have data to use.—Geraldine Tay, mother of four children aged 10, 11, 16, and 16*

Parents would also seek to restrict the nature of their children's social media use and even to actively (and perhaps intrusively) monitor their social media activity:

> *We already said [to Morgan], "We are lending you this phone, so we have the right to check and see." He is very defensive, so I only browse through it in his sleep. But they are so smart. They delete certain messages. Because I peeked when he was chatting with his cousin, then he went to bed. When I checked back, the messages were not there anymore. [I] don't [use Snapchat]. My kids are scared we join [Snapchat] also. I don't really know about that. I am also not familiar with Instagram. He is aware that he spends too much time on Instagram.—Violet Cheung, mother of two sons aged 9 and 15*

REFLECTION

In this chapter, I have sought to outline the familial context in which mobile media are adopted and used. I have also highlighted the broader aspirations that these parents hold for their children's future and the obligations toward their children that they deem paramount, so that the priorities and values that undergird their mobile media use can be fully understood and teased out. In so doing, I offer the sociotechnical backdrop against which transcendent parenting has emerged.

With the trope of parental determinism strengthening over time (Furedi 2002), coupled with long-held Asian conceptions of the duty of parents to imbue their children with the right values to ensure academic excellence (Chao 1995; Chen and Luster 2002), parents in Singapore do see themselves as the key agents of their children's positive growth and development. Their active participation in the minutiae of their children's school lives, from packing their schoolbags to reviewing homework and meeting the teachers, reveals the deep sense of commitment most of them hold toward this aspect of parenting. The assiduous efforts they make in building a wholesome and edifying media environment for their children are another facet of their mission to nurture their children. The important role that mobile communication plays in supporting these efforts was also glimpsed and will be discussed more fully in the subsequent chapters. Indeed, the key to grasping the context that the transcendent parent inhabits is to first understand parents' sense of their role as the principal nurturers of their children, as well as the centrality of the children's academic endeavors in their lives.

4

At School

From among the sea of schoolchildren clustered at the gate, she was able to pick out her son in an instant, recognizing him by his trademark slouch and electric blue backpack. As he piled into the car, he groaned about the homework his teacher had assigned for the day: *"I can't believe Mrs. Prakash wants us to . . ." "Yes, I know, to build a model of the hibiscus flower? I just got the notification on* ClassDojo. *And you have spelling tomorrow too." This was a scene that was played out often. Without even having to check with her son, she was fully cognizant of her son's daily homework and school commitments because of the app that the school had instructed all parents to download. It kept her well apprised of her son's many academic obligations and school activities. She started to mentally plan how he should complete his homework from now until dinnertime.*

Indeed, as I will show in this chapter, the transcendent parent is one who is virtually keeping the child company in the classroom, and there are hosts of technologies to help the parent be omnipresent in their children's school lives. Schools and teachers are employing an ever-widening range of digital and mobile channels for teacher-parent-student communication relating to the child's school life. I first explain how schools are incorporating technology into their

Transcendent Parenting. Sun Sun Lim, Oxford University Press (2020).

DOI: 10.1093/oso/9780190088989.001.0001

communication with parents. I then draw on the experience of parents in Singapore to discuss how the growing use of technologically facilitated parent-teacher communication heralds new benefits but also introduces unprecedented parenting responsibilities. I also show how the mobile-enabled communication climate draws parents ever-more deeply into their children's educational endeavors and consider the implications for parents' well-being and children's personal development.

Communication between teachers and parents about their children is referred to as home-school conferencing and is considered a cornerstone of parental educational involvement. Broadly, home-school conferencing comprises personal communication between the school and parents pertaining specifically to their own children, along with mass communication with parents regarding generic school or class information. The increasingly avid use of mobile communication has seen technology play a greater role in home-school conferencing (Stright and Yeo 2014). For direct communication with parents of a more personalized nature, usually to discuss the individual child's academic performance and/or behavioral and disciplinary issues, teachers have traditionally relied on face-to-face teacher-parent meetings and phone calls. With the growing use of mediated communication, generic messaging apps and social media platforms, such as WhatsApp, Facebook Messenger, and WeChat, are also being used for home-school conferencing among schools worldwide.

Increasingly too, teachers have started to adopt custom, online gradebooks and apps designed specifically for recording and tracking individual children's academic progress, including even forums for open teacher-parent or parent-parent discussions (Morris et al. 2010). These include apps such as ClassDojo, Remind, Edmodo, and SchoolCircle (Wabisabi Learning 2014). Parents can typically utilize these services via an online website and an accompanying mobile app, thereby heightening convenience and accessibility. For mass communication with parents regarding general school or class information, teachers have traditionally used printed notifications, but these are being displaced by methods such as e-mail, text messaging, school websites, and social media (Morris et al. 2010; Pakter and Chen 2013; Thompson, Mazer, and Grady 2015; Zieger and Tan 2012). Clearly, home-school conferencing practices have evolved along with the growing prevalence of online communication and the rising ubiquity of smartphones.

MOBILE-ENABLED TEACHER-PARENT COMMUNICATION

Our respondents were avid users of the apps and services schools have introduced for home-school conferencing. In Singapore, these apps and services are used systematically at the primary and secondary school levels. Many parents welcomed the schools' use of apps to disseminate mass information, such as announcements of events and official reminders, because it helps them engage in more seamless micro-coordination of their children's schedules. They particularly appreciated their immediacy, accessibility, and ease of use:

> *Parents' Gateway is the school's [digital] notice board. They will send any activities coming, any forms they want me to sign. In the past they used hard copies that they passed to the children and the children then passed them to us. I like Parents' Gateway because sometimes my children will miss the hard copy, then I have no notice about the activity. So for all of these, we will receive a notification and key it into our calendar. So you see my calendar is full of their activities. Yes, it helps a lot. And it is also easy for me to trace back, you just click one button, very easy for you to read.—Ho Pei Yi, mother of three daughters aged 6, 8, and 10*

For younger preschool children, who are less adept at transmitting information between the school and the pupils, parents were even more appreciative of the wealth of information they could access about their children's school lives via apps such as Qoqolo:

> *The school started using this app three years ago. So I have all her information from nursery to K2, all the posts, [photo] albums, other things. I find that this app is better [than ClassDojo] because the teacher actually posted other things like spelling lists and all that. ClassDojo is a screenshot, but this one [Qoqolo] the teacher posts the documents here. It's in a Word document, easier to print I think. We can print what are the sight words that they have to learn. When you are free, and you want to recap the old photographs of the child when she was young, you can go back to that folder. And then because they have their meals in the kindergarten, the teachers also posted under announcements like, morning, afternoon, what are the menus. The calendar, what are the happenings in the following month . . . So this is quite organized.—Jenna Chang, mother of two children aged 6 and 9*

Beyond these official school channels, there was a thriving network of parent-to-parent chats on social media platforms that are popular in Singapore, with WhatsApp being the most often mentioned. As with the situation in many other countries, parents in Singapore use these chat groups to interact with parents of other children who attend the same school or class to consult one another on school-related matters. With WhatsApp messages being effectively free, thus allowing users to easily and liberally transmit photographs and videos along with text messages, our respondents shared and received all kinds of school-related information. These spanned the gamut from reminders about homework deadlines, solutions to challenging homework questions, and photographs taken during field trips, to invitations for social events such as playdates and birthday parties. In essence, these different apps emblematized what Nelson (2010) identified as technological aids that parents adopt to maintain active oversight of their children's affairs.

However, these apps were clearly not an unalloyed blessing considering that expectations of parental care have amplified in recent decades (Furedi 2002). In fact, the situation could be rather stressful for respondents with more than one child in school. Parents with multiple children had to maintain numerous chats with teachers and other groups of parents and be active on a diverse panoply of platforms. Hence, some parents admitted to feeling overwhelmed by the sheer proliferation of apps they needed to manage and expressed hopes for greater integration and streamlining for greater ease of management. Different subject teachers would use different platforms, and these were above and beyond the main portals used by the school:

> *I would love it if it's one seamless platform, rather than having to check all three platforms. 'Cos this is one school, but for one school I have to check three apps, it's a bit too much I find. I'd rather go into one app, and these are the things I have to do for Malay, these for maths, and these are the school administrative things, rather than checking between the three. Oh, have I done this already? Have I done that already?—Aaqilah, mother of three daughters aged 4, 6, and 7*
>
> *Not all teachers are using the apps, some use another form of communication: e-mails, calls . . . I don't prefer that. If the teacher is nice, like, for my younger girl, two teachers are using ClassDojo, but the form teacher and the science teacher don't use it, so I have to use SMS (laugh). That's why I said, a lot of forms of communication, channels . . . But [I have] no choice. So now I have to pray hard that I [my child] will get the teacher who is using the app. That's easier.—Yvette Lim, mother of two daughters aged 9 and 13*

At the same time, however, this high level of teacher-parent connectivity created unwelcome pressures for parents as teachers would also contact parents directly about their children's schoolwork, especially if the child was underperforming or encountering disciplinary issues. For example, Geraldine Tay, mother of four children aged 10, 11, 16, and 16, showed us a WhatsApp conversation between her and her 11-year-old son's Chinese-language teacher. Besides first sharing photos of sections of the assignment that the child did not complete, the teacher also exhorted Geraldine to remind her son to behave better in class:

> TEACHER'S TEXT: *Also, I would like to seek your help with talking to him about his behavior in class . . . He will walk around and disturb (sometimes hitting people) teacher and others.*
>
> GERALDINE'S TEXT: *Huh . . . hitting people!! Ok . . . will talk to him later.*

Such direct teacher-parent communication could have an adverse impact on family relationships as they create tension and even trigger confrontations between parents and children that clouded the relationship:

> *I don't really bother [about the apps]. I don't want to stress myself, then I will stress my kids. I am that kind of paranoid person. Last time, for Morgan, when the teacher called, messaged, I would be very panicked [sic] . . . Teachers would e-mail me. Then I would be paranoid, and I would keep asking him because I didn't feel I trusted him so I kept asking him. So he felt mistrust. So that's why he would be angry with me.—Violet Cheung, mother of two sons aged 9 and 15*

As Violet's experience shows, the direct connection she had with her son's teachers created fissures in their mother-son relationship because she would pit the teacher's words against his and demand accountability for his academic performance. Her avid focus on his schoolwork, coupled with her self-admitted paranoia, led her to take the teachers' communications too gravely, and these became a thorny locus in their relationship. When she became conscious of how her son was withdrawing from her as a consequence, she made the concerted decision not to obsess over the home-school conferencing apps so as not to impose further pressure on her son. Her actions and introspection reflect how acutely parents in Asia can perceive the responsibility to raise "high-quality children," as research has found (Yeoh and Huang 2010).

And yet it is difficult for the concerned parent not to be drawn into overseeing their children's schoolwork, particularly when teachers explicitly request parental involvement. ClassDojo messages from teachers would urge the interviewed parents to "help reinforce" curricular content and even to "check your children's schoolbag and handbook, remind them to complete their homework, and submit [the homework] on time."

Some respondents did find such reminders stressful, as one lamented:

> *If you hear from the Chinese [language] teachers, you know there's something you need to work on already. The teacher will usually call me, "You know, Martin [her son] needs to improve on his writing, his oral. Martin didn't do his homework." So if I don't hear from the Chinese teacher, it's very good news.—Gilian Lau, mother of two children aged 8 and 12*

Indeed, some parents would use the apps to micro-manage their children's school issues. The easy accessibility of mobile devices provided direct parent-teacher connections and the additional convenience of capturing images of their children's assignments. Hence, parents could be considerably more involved in their children's school matters than if these digital infrastructures did not exist. For instance, mother Lisa Lin contacted her 10-year-old son's English teacher via ClassDojo messages to establish the correct spelling for a word for which he was marked wrong in the spelling test. Upon clarification she then proceeded to confirm with the teacher that because he had actually spelled the word correctly, there was no need for him to submit corrections.

Similarly, Esther Lee wrote the following message to her 11-year-old son's teacher: "Hi Mrs. XXX, Charlie asked me to inform you that he had done his compo[sition] correction in pen. He's sorry he had forgotten that he had to do it in pencil." These seemingly trifling matters, which the children themselves could have sought to clarify with their teachers, involved parental interventions that may in part have robbed the children of their sense of autonomy, agency, and self-representation. At the same time, do such micro-practices serve to set the norm that parental involvement of this level is both desired and desirable, further burdening and ossifying the "cultural script" (Faircloth 2014, 31) around ideal parenting?

Our respondents thus negotiated many tensions between wanting to be involved in their children's academic endeavors and resisting the urge to become *too* involved. This was especially so with younger children in primary school who were less aware of the goings-on in these apps that their parents were using for school-related matters. In such cases, parents would deliberately withhold the knowledge of these apps from their children for fear of inculcating a dependency:

> *I cannot give Oscar [seven-years-old, primary 1] the app [ClassDojo], 'cos if he knows of the app, he will know that the teacher gives me these things [examples of homework answers] directly. He doesn't know that I use it as a backup. Because if he knows, he will not pay attention in class, and we want him to pay attention in the classroom. Otherwise he will think, "My mom knows everything."—Amanda Tan, mother of two sons aged 4 and 7*

Our respondents were thus often torn between helping their children with homework to ensure that they could keep up with their peers and refraining from extending their assistance to allow their children to develop independence.

> *So at home, it's his duty to open his schoolbag. I won't touch his schoolbag. So he has to open the schoolbag on his own, to check what's inside. So if there's no homework, we will just take it as having no homework. But actually in the background, I would have known whether there's homework or not. Maybe I just prompt him, "Did you check your file? Is it there?" Oh yeah, it's there! But once, he claimed there was no homework, I knew that there was homework, but I let him go to school and face the consequences.—Amanda Tan, mother of two sons aged 4 and 7*

MOBILE-ENABLED PARENT-PARENT COMMUNICATION

Parent-parent communication constituted another critical dimension of parental involvement in children's school lives. These usually took place over messaging apps, such as WhatsApp and Facebook Messenger, with the former being more often mentioned. Parents expressed a grudging acceptance of WhatsApp parent groups because they offer a helpful, failsafe channel for urgent clarifications about homework, school events, and instructions from teachers. As this mother explained:

> *So for Jake [11-years-old, primary 5], we have constant communication with his classmates' parents because, you know, the teachers sometimes do not tell you the information, and some information*

you will need quite fast, like the spelling list, or what to bring for tomorrow's camping trip. So we just double-check with the friends, or WhatsApp the parents, "Do you have this thing that I need?"—Geraldine Tay, mother of four children aged 10, 11, 15, and 16

On the one hand, parents expressed a reluctance to rely too heavily on these groups as a crutch for their children, who would then not bother to develop ownership of their individual responsibilities as a student. On the other hand, parents were also clearly reassured by the presence of these WhatsApp groups as a valuable last resort when their children overlooked any important instructions. Working parents, too, mentioned that the stay-at-home mothers would send out alerts about school instructions right after school and this helped the parents who were still at work to have a sense of what to expect from their children when they got home. Indeed, one could say that the parents' very involvement in these group chats was also a manifestation of concerted cultivation (Lareau 2003), marshaling all available resources to better pave the way for their children's educational endeavors.

Notably however, some parents did find the sheer volume of notifications from teachers and other parents inundating and developed strategies to manage the flood of information:

So those [working parents] in the office will receive a lot of "ping," "ping," "ping" (laugh). Unless they set the [WhatsApp group] chat to "silent." Because there were over one hundred photos [of the school excursion] that the parent volunteer would help to post. So far nobody left this group. I think 'cos it's active participation in your child's school life. If parents are not happy, they can just log off or something. I mute it. It's too many messages. It's quite distracting because sometimes I need to do other things.—Jenna Chang, mother of two children aged 6 and 9

I disabled the notifications, I don't want to be bothered like every time my phone goes "Ping! Ping! Ping!" I will check the apps when I have the time. I don't really like the notification sounds. I will feel that I have to do it now. I would rather do it at my own time.—Aaqilah, mother of three daughters aged 4, 6, and 7

On a more extreme end, some parents were observed to use such platforms to complain about the school or its teachers, and to mobilize other parents to protest against school policies or practices they disagreed with, in a kind of technologically charged, mobile-accelerated form of concerted cultivated (Lareau 2003):

Previously under the last principal, she was very ambitious, so the kids had a lot of remedial lessons . . . the school was very driven, KPI-focused, it was like [having] sales targets. So it was very competitive. But this new principal is very different. He is more well-rounded so he changed a few things in the school, which for parents who are very ambitious, they do not like. In the chat group, they started talking: "Why is it that this year they start streaming [students according to different abilities]?" But usually I just ignore them. I do not see the point in such a discussion. I do not know them personally, so it is not productive to get into an argument.—Samantha Sun, mother of three children aged 4, 6, and 11

So the concern of some of the mommies was the class was too big for two teachers to handle. So they like to discuss among themselves first, before they bring attention to any issue to the teachers. I find this constructive, when they get together and they find, "Hey is it just me? Am I alone on this?" Then some mommies are like, "No you are not alone." So as a group, we bring it up to the teachers. But I spoke to the teacher, who said "You know, I'd rather the parents just come to me straight, rather than they discuss as a group. If you have any concerns, just come to me, rather than as a group." Maybe they try to get more numbers to get support as a group. Not so good, I guess, for the teacher. When they are in big numbers, they get intimidating.—Aaqilah, mother of three daughters aged 4, 6, and 7

This level of heightened communication among parents also had ramifications for parental expectations of children's academic performance, at times translating into a perceived intensification of peer pressure:

Because of improved communication in the parents' networks, because in the past there was little communication between the parents unless you met up for tea, or you purposely picked them in school to see them . . . Now, we don't even step out of the house, and I know what's happening, so it's like, "Oh, so and so already studied," or they show a note, "Oh, this is how we prepare our notes." Usually we give thumbs up, we don't put down others. Sometimes it will become peer pressure, somehow it will become a chain reaction that indirectly will build up the expectations on our kids.—Sophie Chua, mother of two children aged 10 and 11

I heard from my colleagues and friends that other parents will compare. I think the information is too much! Too much! For example, like, for PSLE,[1] *they will have a WhatsApp group, then they will have all sorts of things. Like* "kiasu" *[Hokkien for afraid to lose out] parents, they will share a lot of things. I don't want to have that kind of pressure or stress because I will put that stress on my children! So, I don't want to pressure them. To avoid all this [excessive information], I don't join parents' WhatsApp groups. If I need clarifications, I check with teachers, it's better because it's the most accurate*

1. Primary School Leaving Examination—the crucial examination that all primary school children in Singapore take in primary 6 at the age of 12 to determine which secondary school they can enter.

> *information. So for me, I'd rather be out of the parents' groups. I've got friends who are quite* kiasu, *they will join parents' groups. I know that it can be quite stressful because these parents will start to compare. They will start to send the kid to a lot of enrichment classes. I don't like that.—Yvette Lim, mother of two daughters aged 9 and 13*

For parents who actively participate in or follow such chats, these WhatsApp groups become a virtual embodiment of the peer pressure in parenting, where norms, social comparisons, competition, and rivalries are performed and articulated in a highly visible manner. As Furedi (2008) noted, parenting can resemble competitive sports! In fact, some respondents recounted how parents would jockey to volunteer for activities and share what they were doing to boost their children's academic efforts. Arguably, the intensity and permanence of interactions on these mediated groups makes such pressures more palpable and perceptible than in fleeting face-to-face interactions.

Along with the additional pressure, some parents were also aggrieved about the diminished sense of responsibility that such communication may foster in children. They expressed concerns that their children will thereby devolve their learning and obligations to their parents and teachers. At the same time, they felt that some parents in turn shifted their own responsibility to other parents whom they leaned on as a reliable fall back for school-related information. They excoriated such parents for failing to exercise personal ownership over their children's academic work:

> *Parents over-rely on the apps. I mean, apps like this did not exist during our time, [and yet] every day our homework was still just fine. If you did not do it, you were punished. I prefer it that way, personally. I do not enjoy the apps. I find them annoying. I do not see why there needs to be so much communication. I think it is unnecessary. I actually prefer the communication to be kept to the students and then,*

> *there is a greater sense of responsibility. Because of all these apps, the students know that the teachers will WhatsApp my mom, and they are very hands-off. In the WhatsApp group there will be a lot of parents who will keep asking about what the homework for today is, and to me, your kids should know . . . There are times when at nine forty-five p.m., a parent can be like, "Is there spelling tomorrow? What is the list?" To me, it is stupid because it shows that you are not interested, you do not care, and your child does not, either. I mean, children need to have a sense of ownership, otherwise they never learn responsibility.—Isabel Tong, mother of one daughter aged 7*

Yet, even as other parents acknowledged that they and their children had developed dependency on these apps, they also felt that the apps were a necessary evil because of the high stakes at play in their children's education. They sensed that the heavy use of these apps for educational matters significantly ramped up parental involvement in children's school lives, thus exacerbating the level of competition among children, to the point that those whose parents were not using these apps would fall behind their peers:

> *Actually I feel that somehow this app does really spoon-feed them. Spoon-feeds the parents. In the eighties, when we were in school, we didn't have this kind of knowledge, so we relied on the child. But now, it's like the school is spoon-feeding the parents, then the parents must spoon-feed the children (laugh). In a way, good and bad. Because now the dynamic of education is totally different. Yes, [my son] definitely relies on me, but he still does his homework because everyone is doing it. If I totally ignore, totally log off from ClassDojo, or I totally leave the WhatsApp group, I won't know what's happening. What will the consequences be? He will be behind schedule. Everybody, every parent has downloaded these!—Jenna Chang, mother of two children aged 6 and 9*

One respondent had even observed other parents who leveraged the seamless mobile connections to usurp the children's responsibilities. One mother communicated directly with other parents to parcel out project work to the different children in the group and offered to integrate everyone's contributions (see Figure 4.1):

> *One parent took over! "You do the three slides, you do the three slides, then send to me then I will consolidate!" Then I said, "Where is the kid's role in all this?" Then we started to discuss. Then some people agreed, then blah blah blah . . . it went on and on. And the reason why she wanted to start assigning [homework] was because she was going on holiday. She was making decisions for the kids!*—Esther Lee, mother of three children aged 5, 11, and 13

Indeed, many parents admitted to feeling that the parent group chats amplified their feelings of responsibility toward the children's academic obligations, thereby also reflecting strong perceptions of parental determinism (Furedi 2008):

> *With the WhatsApp group for the parents, I really feel that I also go to school with them. We have to pay a lot of attention, what is the homework every day, so we are also part of their studies. I have had this feeling from quite some time ago.*—Ho Pei Yi, mother of three daughters aged 6, 8, and 10
>
> *In Chinese there's a phrase*—"peidu mama" *[mother who accompanies her child to study]. Now we even say, "Hey, exam is coming." It's like MY exam is coming. We are talking as if WE are sitting for the exam! It becomes us. In a way, we feel very attached [to the apps]. If we don't have the apps, we don't know what is happening in school, we don't get that feeling, that kind of vibe. With these apps, we are constantly moving with the kids. Even their camps, where they go, the teacher sends updates . . . Good thing is we are*

Figure 4.1 WhatsApp parents' group chat with parents discussing children's group project.

aligned with the kids. But sometimes we need to let go. Sometimes I think, "Crazy! Why am I so involved? Why am I feeling the exam panic?"—Joan Tan, mother of three children aged 7, 11, and 13

GRADEBOOK APPS

Most of our respondents also relied heavily on teacher-parent communication apps, such as ClassDojo, for personalized information about their children's academic performance and updates on in-class activities. Previous research has found distinct benefits of such gradebooks. Parents who are given access to online gradebooks are more likely to take the initiative to speak to their children and the teacher about the child's academic performance (Zieger and Tan 2012). This is indeed preferable to the situation where teachers initiate conversations with parents only when the child has an academic or behavioral issue (Blackerby Jr. 2005). Hence, universal provision of online gradebook access can help boost parental involvement in children's education regardless of whether children are facing particular concerns in school.

For our respondents with children in primary school in particular, their children's teachers would enlist such apps to provide detailed instructions to parents on specific assignments. Some would also include information on the overall performance of the class so that parents could see where their own children stood relative to their peers. As Figures 4.2 and 4.3 clearly indicate, the teachers used the app to provide pointers on a recent test and both the maximum and median scores were also shared to help the parent gauge their child's performance relative to their peers.

It is likely that the teachers were fundamentally well-intentioned and were using such messages to encourage their students to do better. But such information on the overall class performance can exacerbate

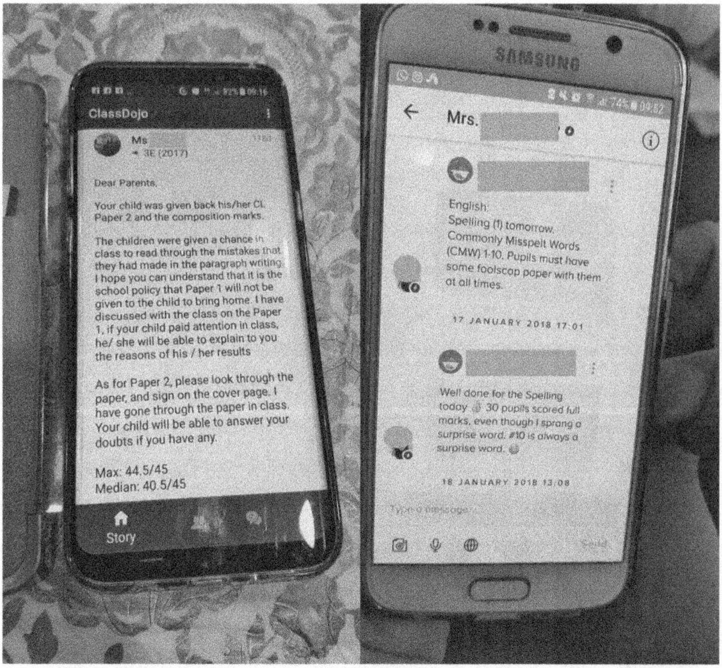

Figures 4.2 and 4.3 ClassDojo (*left*) and Remind (*right*); messages from teachers to parents with information on students' performance in recent assessments and tests.

feelings of competitiveness and make parents more inclined to benchmark their children's performance against those of their classmates, inadvertently contributing to peer pressure. As shown in Figure 4.3, the teacher commended the class by saying: "Well done for the spelling today. 30 pupils scored full marks, even though I sprang a surprise word. No. 10 is always a surprise word." If the average class has between 30 to 35 pupils, how would the small minority that did not attain the perfect score feel?

Teachers would also use these apps to get parents more involved in the child's classroom learning by notifying parents of the rewards they had given the children for their in-class performance. Through such information, parents would glean insights into the child's classroom experience, using it as a departure point to find out more from the child:

> *Oscar [7-years-old, primary 1] is very curious about his teacher's feedback to him in class every day, so he will come home and ask me to check ClassDojo for his performance in class, whether the teacher has given him a star. Last week he had something: "Kind and helping someone." So he was very happy that he was rewarded by the teacher. Whereas, in WhatsApp, you can't reward the child. On ClassDojo there's a summary of his performance I can track over time. It's documented well. ClassDojo does give me peace of mind. So whether he is good or not good, I get regular feedback. I don't feel very distant. I feel that I am following my son into the classroom, although I am not in the classroom.—Amanda Tan, mother of two sons aged 4 and 7*
>
> *My daughter had just entered primary one, and I was a new parent, so I just wanted to know everything. Very curious. At that time her teacher liked to give marks to my daughter. I wanted to know how many marks she scored. I checked ClassDojo more often. 'Cos every time the teacher gave marks, she would say, "Plus five for taking part in the discussion, plus five for neat handwriting." So I knew what was happening.—Low Ting Ting, mother of two daughters aged 8 and 10*

For such respondents, the ClassDojo app gave them the assurance that their children were flourishing in school because the child's in-class performance, while previously inaccessible, was now quantified and served to the parent, becoming a de facto proxy monitoring tool. As reflected in both mothers' accounts, these parents were eager to understand how their children were faring in school and were gratified by such insights and feedback, manifesting their desire to engage in concerted cultivation (Lareau 2003). However, there are concerns about the child's right to privacy, with experts urging parents not to use these online gradebooks to spy on their children but as a pathway to discussing with their children what happens in school (Zieger and Tan 2012).

Another way teachers used such apps to offer parents glimpses into the classroom was through sharing photographs of activities the children undertake in school. Parents lauded such photographs for boosting their understanding of their children's classroom experiences, enabling them to more effectively support their children's learning:

> *The teacher regularly posts pictures of what the class does every day. So when I go through the homework with him at home, it makes things a lot easier, 'cos I know what he is learning in school.—Amanda Tan, mother of two sons aged 4 and 7*

Involved parents would thus use such apps and features to vicariously experience their children's school days, from praise and rewards by the teacher to the learning activities the children participated in. Again, the depth with which parents can learn of and participate in their children's school lives is heightened by such digital infrastructures.

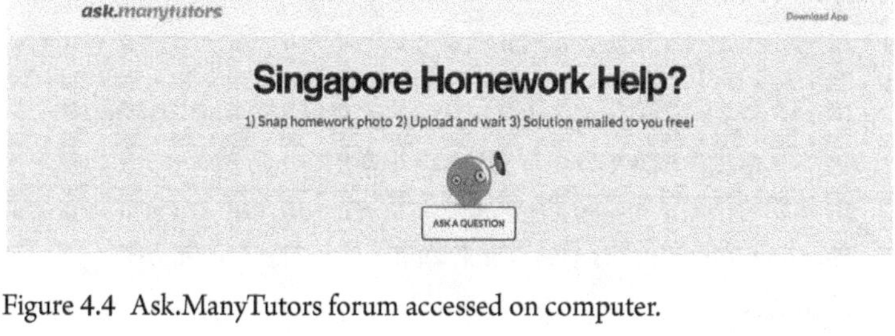

Figure 4.4 Ask.ManyTutors forum accessed on computer.

HOMEWORK HELPER APPS

As the children ascend the school ladder, homework invariably becomes far more challenging, straining parents' abilities to guide their children. In response, "homework helper" websites and apps that offer free online tutelage have emerged to cater to such demands. For example, many respondents mentioned the popular Many Tutors app which has an Ask.ManyTutors forum where students can upload a picture of their assignment and receive an answer. This free supplementary service on the app helps raise awareness of the core Many Tutors service that offers listings for private tutors who advertise their services there (see Figure 4.4 for the Ask.ManyTutors forum interface).

Many of our participants lauded the utility of such "homework helper" services that offer support with the benefit of anonymity:

> *Ask.ManyTutors is good, that means they [our children] can learn if we need help and there is nobody there to help. I tell her [my daughter] to check with her teacher, but she is shy. The teacher says, if you need help we can WhatsApp her, but she is uncomfortable to WhatsApp her teacher.—Iris Ching, mother of three children aged 10, 12, and 14*

Direct mobile connectivity with other parents also makes it easy for parents to solicit help when their children encounter difficulties with homework:

> *Yes [when my children were in primary school] I just asked friends for help. Then, problem solved! I just sent to my friends, then my friends would help me, draw out the mathematical model, that kind of thing. That easy. Over WhatsApp.—Judy Lau, mother of two children aged 11 and 14*

Given the perceived high costs of their children's underperformance, and many parents' commitment to ensuring that their children succeed academically, these "homework helpers" were welcomed as a definite boon. The ability to tap the wisdom of professional tutors or other parents gave these parents the assurance that they always had someone to turn to in circumstances where they were unable to help their own children. This capacity to support their children in their academic endeavors was something many parents took very seriously as exemplified by this mother's perspective:

> *When it comes to examinations, my son starts worrying whether he has prepared enough, has done enough, things like that. If not for his worrying, I don't think I have that much of a problem. Maths is not getting easier. So a lot of the time I think my stress is due to like "Go and study on his behalf." Like I said, I Google, I watch videos. So what I do, I usually go to YouTube. I signed up for a Facebook group called "Learning out of the Box Maths Skills Group (for Parents)." I have to equip myself with a lot of tools in order to help my son do better or my kids do better.—Melissa Loh, mother of three children aged 6, 9, and 11*

These parents are clearly driven by a strong sense of ownership over their children's learning and they proactively marshal as wide a range of resources as possible. Our respondents expressed the fervent hope that through their active interventions, they could give their children the necessary support to help them thrive in this competitive academic environment.

REFLECTION

The growing multitude of ways in which parents can be connected to their children's teachers and to other parents, and the mediated platforms by which parents can be directly involved in their children's learning, have created vast possibilities for transcendent parenting. The seamlessness of teacher-parent communication has drawn parents ever more tightly into their children's school lives, being constantly apprised of the latest assignments and tests. The rich environment of exchange between parents creates a culture of sharing but also oversharing, such that parents may feel that they are constantly on their toes, straining to keep up with other parents and children. Gradebook apps that offer peeks into the child's classroom experience and evaluations of their participation during lessons allow parents to virtually sit by their children's side even as the latter enter the classroom on their own. In the words of mother Amanda Tan, "I feel that I am in the classroom with my son, although I am not in the classroom." As well, in the face of challenging assignments, parents can mobilize external assistance from homework helper apps or other parents to provide tutelage and support to their children. The transcendent parent is therefore one who must navigate this rich communication and information milieu as they strive to excel at their parenting duties to help their children thrive academically.

As my findings show, the accessibility, frequency, and intensity of communication in our mobile media-infused climate keep parents constantly reminded of their children's educational tasks. By extension, parents find it challenging to divest themselves of such responsibilities, thinking about their children's academic matters while they are at work, and managing their homework well after the children are in bed. The competitive educational landscape seems to have found new vitality in parents' chat groups, allowing peer comparisons to be undertaken and peer pressure to be exerted and experienced in unprecedented ways. Indeed, transcendent parenting is characterized by a certain relentlessness, requiring that parents are omnipresent in their children's school lives, thus introducing a new dimension to the phenomena of intensive parenting (Hays 1996), concerted cultivation (Lareau 2003), and parenting out of control (Nelson 2010), while also aggravating the parenting time famine (Furedi 2008).

5

Out and About

As he stepped out of his office into the hot midday sun to meet a friend for lunch, he received a notification on his phone from the Companion app. It had sent him a request from his daughter to "keep her company" as she walked back to her apartment in New Haven where she was on a college exchange program. He was by now familiar with this routine as there would be times when she joined her friends for late events, but no one else was headed in her direction at the end of the night. With this app, even though it was 1 a.m. for her in New Haven and 1 p.m. for him in Singapore, he could "accompany" her and sound the alarm if the need arose. And he could be assured that she was fine, even across the miles.

With the intensifying use of mobile communication, families are now linked through multiple mobile connections. These offer a rich palette of aural, visual, and video channels to convey everything from transactional exchanges to emotionally charged messages, across the asynchronous to virtually synchronous to fully synchronous spectrum. Indeed, it is the powerful combination of rich social and audiovisual cues and synchronicity that have made mobile communication an indispensable tool in the parental surveillance

Transcendent Parenting. Sun Sun Lim, Oxford University Press (2020).

DOI: 10.1093/oso/9780190088989.001.0001

assemblage. There is an extensive slate of mobile communication features, customized apps and services that parents now actively tap to monitor their children's whereabouts or to simply have a sense of their well-being.

Back in 2003 when basic feature phones were in widespread use, I studied the technology use of middle-class families in China and Korea to understand how these devices were influencing communication within connected households. The mothers I interviewed lamented that the mobile phone had enhanced their connectivity to their children but also raised the levels of anxiety they experienced as parents. As one mother explained:

> *At first, I thought having the mobile phone would be so convenient because you can always contact each other. But when the mobile phone signal is weak and you can't get through [to your children], you feel so anxious. Before we had the mobile phone and we weren't able to contact them, we just didn't think about it. But with the mobile phone, sometimes they're not contactable, the phone is turned off or you're not in a networked area . . . It stresses me to death!—Mother, 39, Manager, Family 1, Beijing* (Lim and Soon 2010)

Hence, this state of perpetual contact (Katz and Aakhus 2002) was effectively a state of perpetual concern for their children's well-being and evoked in these parents mixed feelings about technology. Whereas parents were previously unable to personally supervise their children at all times, this new-found reassurance brought about by a constant digital connection can be welcome. And yet, this veneer of reassurance can become a specter of persistent responsibility that induces unwelcome stress and feelings of disquiet when the digital connection becomes unstable or if it conveys a panicky call from the child.

With a premium placed in Asian societies on parental oversight and supervision, parents feel duty bound to supervise their children's behavior and their peer interactions to avert risky activity. In this chapter, I show how the transcendent parent, constantly tethered to their children via a dense array of mobile connections, can seek to "accompany" and "watch over" their children everywhere they go. Whether their children are by their side or out of sight, these parents can still train a concerned gaze on them, thereby shielding them from any dangers and risks they believe could arise. This practice has been further invigorated by the increasingly sophisticated uses of mobile communication, such as remote surveillance cameras or location-tracking services that allow parents to exercise oversight. Ultimately, these innovations traffic in the notion that as long as we can monitor our children, appointed caregivers, and their immediate environment, parents can enhance, if not ensure, our children's safety.

Closedcircuit television (CCTV) cameras that allow parents to observe live-in nannies at home, webcams that enable parents to peer into the preschool classroom, wearable tracking devices or mobile phone apps that help parents pinpoint their children's physical location—these are all means by which parents can keep watch over children even when they are not within their immediate vicinity. In this regard, the zeal and instinct to ensure that children are well looked after when they are in the care of others may be energized or even amplified by the technologies that enable remote surveillance of children and their appointed caregivers. I examine how this emergence of apps, devices, and services that heighten parental oversight strongly resonates with the proclivity toward close supervision of children in many Asian societies, thus further intensifying transcendent parenting practices. I also explore how parents perceive and use these services, and how these may have influenced their relationships with their children.

REMOTE SURVEILLANCE SERVICES

In the era of transcendent parenting, how are children digitally connected to their parents across all ages? In their preschool years, children are unable to fend for themselves and need to be under direct adult supervision. With the rise in double-income families that increasingly outsource caregiving to individuals or institutions, a slew of technological innovations has been developed to help parents exercise remote supervision over their preschool children and their caregivers. Such innovations range from infant monitors in childhood to mobile phones in adolescence (Nelson 2010).

For preschoolers, such innovations would include webcams that enable parents to literally keep an eye on their children. CCTVs are increasingly installed in preschools in Singapore, to the point that some parenting advice sites recommend checking the school's policy on reviewing CCTV footage as a criterion for selection (Tan 2017). Separately, a mobile app was introduced to allow parents to monitor their children's school bus rides via notifications sent to their phones. The School Bus Management System provides every child with a small electronic tag so that bus drivers are alerted when a child boards or alights from the bus. It also sends parents phone notifications when their children have arrived safely in school, while enabling them to track the location of the bus. The Chairman of the Singapore School Transport Association championed the virtues of the system, proclaiming that "even when parents are overseas, they get notifications on their child's whereabouts" (*The Straits Times* 2016). This surveillance system also includes four internal cameras that capture the behavior of the driver and the passengers. Furthermore, the system tracks the bus's movement and location and triggers alerts to central command if it diverges from its customary route or if the driver exceeds the speed limit.

Beyond such institutional settings, even domestic spaces can be easily retrofitted with remote surveillance systems. One notable trend in Asia is the installation of webcams for families who hire live-in helpers to care for their children. There have been several high-profile incidents in several countries where parents discovered their children being subjected to physical abuse after scrutinizing videos or watching live feeds of hidden CCTV cameras they had installed in their homes. In Singapore for example, a domestic helper was jailed for two weeks after her employers viewed footage on their CCTV camera that revealed her physical abuse of their 14-month-old son (Hussain 2016). Unable to get him to sleep, she vented her frustrations by pulling him up by his arm, holding him upside down by his ankles, slapping him, and pushing his head. Similarly, in China, a nanny in Hunan Province was seen via home surveillance camera forcing her one-year-old charge to her breast, slapping his face, and hitting him with a broom (Chen 2017).

While such incidents typically ignite a firestorm of debate over the growing reliance on domestic help to mind children, the media discourse surrounding such incidents seems to regard remote surveillance by parents as part and parcel of parenting. Seldom is mention made of the privacy intrusions such surveillance imposes on the helpers, for the sheer reason that parental oversight is deemed desirable and even sensible. Advice proffered by websites that cater to parenting needs tends to suggest various strategies parents must employ to optimize remote oversight. For example, Asia's leading parenting portal the Asianparent suggests that Wi-Fi enabled CCTV cameras be installed in communal areas of the home and that the helper be instructed to only care for children in those areas to facilitate monitoring. It also recommends being upfront with the helper about the use of these CCTV cameras, stressing that such an approach will motivate the domestic helper to perform better: "She will also be aware that she is being watched at all times and thus, she will do her best to take care of your children" (theAsianparent Singapore n.d.).

Such sensibilities were certainly reflected in the views of some interviewees. As Samantha Sun, a mother to two preschoolers articulated:

> *Yes, the CCTV is a good idea. It protects all parties involved. For infants and young kids who are unable to talk, it deters abusive behavior. When there is a dispute, and it's one person's word against another, there is independent proof. The CCTV is limited as it can only be viewed real time or post-fact and can only cover limited areas, but it's useful. I hear that in China, CCTV is used so extensively in public areas that petty thefts and crime have dropped drastically.*

For her, the vulnerability of young children coupled with the transactional nature with which she views her relationship with appointed caregivers warrants the use of such privacy-invading technologies. Apart from the CCTV camera being critical for furnishing evidence should points of contention arise, she seems to believe that it serves as an effective panoptic device that can discipline the caregiver and prevent unwelcome transgressions. As shared by Jenna Chang, mother of two children aged 6 and 9, "as a courtesy I would inform the maid [domestic helper] about the webcams around and the reason they are installed. This allows her to be more conscious of her own actions and consequences."

Principally, parents were more motivated to install webcams or CCTV cameras if they hired domestic helpers and if their children were of preschool age. As domestic workers are typically low-skilled employees with no formal training in childcare, and were largely regarded as strangers to the household, parents saw the CCTV camera as a useful safeguard for ensuring the well-being of their children. However, parents were less enthused about the use of CCTV cameras in institutional settings such as daycare centers and schools because of the potential adverse impact they could have on teachers and the quality of their teaching. As Jenna Chang, a mother to a 6-year-old preschooler explained:

> *I personally feel that for kindergarten, it is not required to have CCTV or webcams around. Firstly, I trust her teachers. Secondly, I feel that it is an intrusion of privacy for the teachers. Lastly, having such devices might cripple the creativity of the teachers, and they cannot truly be themselves if they know that their every move is being watched.*

To such parents, the presence of such surveillance devices inhibited them from forging a relationship of trust with the teachers and could also undermine the latter's sense of professionalism and self-actualization. Furthermore, the transparency with which teachers conduct themselves also vested confidence in parents. As Evelyn Yau, a homemaker with one preschooler emphatically stated:

> *No, no, and no! I think we should respect the professionalism of teachers and keep webcams out of the school and classroom! Also currently the teachers do send pictures occasionally of what my child is doing, so that for me is sufficient! For teachers to have CCTV in their classrooms will be quite intrusive, unless they themselves request it, but personally I'm against it.*

With the trend toward dual-income, middle-class families in metropolitan Asia hiring live-in help, there is growing demand among parents for surveillance technologies that seemingly afford them greater peace of mind. Even as these webcams and CCTV cameras seem to offer a viable channel for parents to check on their children's well-being, they also create additional burdens for parents to strategically marshal and domesticate these technologies. Parents need to manage the expectations of appointed caregivers around the use of such surveillance measures and to also ensure their smooth functioning, failing which tensions could be introduced to the household. Fundamentally though, even while such services enable parents to transcend the multiple environments their children transit through in their absence, they also expand the ambit of parental responsibility and complicate its nature.

LOCATION-TRACKING SERVICES

The situation alters somewhat as children enter middle childhood or preadolescence around the ages of 9 to 12. They develop an independent existence outside of the home and are likely to become more active in school and with after-school activities. As the child becomes increasingly mature, more parents are prepared to have their children step out independently and to take public transport and attend social gatherings on their own. While the need for parents to exercise oversight either directly or virtually is much reduced, parents nonetheless wish to maintain some form of connection with their children. Consequently, this is when increasing numbers of parents begin to give their children personal mobile phones to facilitate coordination. Mobile phones can also provide parents with a sense of security that their child is safer because she can be contacted or can reach out to the parent in instances of distress or need. For children of this age group, webcams and location trackers thus make way for personally owned and personally toted mobile phones that parents acquire for them.

Whereas earlier generation feature phones merely enabled parents and children to call or text each other, often to check on each other's whereabouts or simply to micro-coordinate activities, the emergence of smartphones with their Global Positioning System (GPS) features has introduced a rich variety of innovations that enables parents and children to be connected in many ways. Quite apart from parents and children being able to stay in touch via voice calls and messaging platforms, such as WhatsApp and LINE, a slew of new apps has been developed for the express purpose of tracking another individual's physical location. For example, apps such as PhoneSheriff can monitor children via their phones through tracking their GPS locations, including even their calling and texting activity as well as the items they download. The phone can also be locked remotely by the parent if the child does not behave (Tahnk 2013). App developers have responded rather enthusiastically to such "needs," even creating more perceived needs through their active marketing of apps.

Within Asia, such location-tracking apps have also proliferated and diffused rapidly as statistics on app downloads indicate. According to AppAnnie (n.d.), as of October 2017, of the top-20 grossing parenting apps in the Google Play store for Singapore, three were for location tracking, including Find My Kids: Child Locator (#9), Family GPS Tracker & Chat + Baby Monitor Online (#11), Find My Kids—GPS Tracker (#20) (see Table 5.1).

The top-ranked child-locator app in both Hong Kong and Singapore, the Find My Kids: Child Locator app claims in its description: "It gives you the most up-to-date information to find people and provides family security" (Google Play, Find My Kids: Child Locator n.d.). And apart from tracking the child's movements, it also enables you to check the battery level on your child's phone so that you can be certain of the phone's last location before its battery power is depleted. Similarly, the Family GPS Tracker + Baby Monitor Online app offers similar services while also trumpeting an additional one: "Now you can listen to what is happening around the child in secret from him. For example, to find out what your nanny is doing at home or how the teacher talks to your child at school. And maybe you have

Table 5.1 CHILD LOCATION-TRACKING APPS AMONG TOP-20 GROSSING PARENTING APPS IN GOOGLE PLAY STORE

Country	*Names and ranks of tracking apps on Google Play's free parenting apps section*
Hong Kong	Find My Kids: Child Locator (#9) Family GPS Tracker & Chat + Baby Monitor Online (#11) Find My Kids—GPS Tracker (#20)
Indonesia	Bosco Parent—Family Safety & Locator (#20)
Singapore	Find My Kids: Child locator (#9) Family GPS Tracker & Chat + Baby Monitor Online (#11) Find My Kids—GPS Tracker (#20)
Thailand	Family Locator & GPS Tracker (#8) GeoZilla GPS Locator—Find Family & Friends (#12)

suspicions that your child is involved a [*sic*] bad company?" They further recommend that their app be used by "[p]arents whose children aged 5–17 walk in the city streets to a kindergarten, school, visit relatives, walk with friends and family members every day." (Google Play, Family GPS Tracker + Baby Monitor Online n.d.) These apps tend to be marketed with similar strategies: manufacturing parental fear to stoke the parental instinct to surveil, and thus deliberately calculated to induce anxieties.

In other parts of the world, criticism has certainly been leveled against location-tracking services such as the Life360 app. Popular in the United States for allowing family members to keep abreast of each other's whereabouts, previous research has noted that developers of such apps deliberately exploit parents' concerns about their children's safety to stimulate demand for such services. They argue that such apps capitalize on parents' sense of duty by inflating risks, offering a false sense of security, and framing surveillance and the control of significant others as desirable and valuable (Hasinoff 2017; Simpson 2014). The manufacturers then seek to quell the anxieties they trigger by presenting neat technological solutions where parents can track whether their children are in locations clearly demarcated as safe or risky. In doing so, any reservations about refraining from "helicopter parenting" and respecting individual privacy are cast aside in the interest of greater peace of mind. Parents are thus sold the myth that by assiduously tracking their children's location via these apps, they can reduce or even eradicate all risks for their children.

Such marketing discourse can resonate with parents who have such anxieties, particularly when their children are crossing milestones in life. For example, Joan Tan is a mother of a 13-year-old boy entering high school and commuting to school on his own. To smoothen this transition, his parents gave him a smartphone and installed the Safe Lagoon app on it as well:

> *When I installed the app, [my son] knows about the app. This app is to monitor where he is going. I will know what time he leaves home. There's a "location" [option] here where I can set the details, then it will alert me. Of course I can manage other locations. The most important is his journey from the train station to school, I want to know that he is safe from home to school. Of course he doesn't really like [the app], but we told him, "This app is not permanent, we installed this because everything is new, you are taking the train on your own, you are taking the phone now," and you know how they [children] get obsessed with phone chats.*

However, of all our respondents, only a small minority had installed such location-tracking apps. Among the few respondents who had deployed such apps, the response within the household was unenthusiastic, even if they could appreciate the rationale. This was reflected in the view of Violet Cheung, a 45-year-old mother to two sons, one aged 15 attending secondary school and another aged 9 attending primary school, and whose husband had installed the Life360 app on her phone and that of her elder son:

> *Safety-wise, daddy has set this [Life360]. Daddy even tracks me also. I don't like it too (laugh). Actually, it's for convenience. Daddy is worried about traffic, starting from this year.*

One reason for the relatively poor adoption of location-tracking services was their cost, as well as their heavy reliance on mobile data. In order to keep their children's smartphone usage in check, respondents with children in primary school tended to give their children older phones with limited functionality or restrict them to very basic data plans or none at all. This was the strategy adopted by Low Ting Ting, a 40-year-old mother of a 10-year-old and an 8-year-old girl, both of whom were in primary school:

> *Definitely, yes, I prefer something like knowing whether [my children] are in school or not. They are taking public buses to school and go home by themselves. Sometimes, after school, I ask them to have lunch first then go home, then they will say, "I want to stay longer in school to do homework." Actually I don't know whether they are playing with friends or staying in school for homework. There was a time when they were supposed to reach home at about one, two-thirty. At four o'clock they still did not reach home. I was a bit nervous because I didn't know where they were. That's why I gave them the phone, but only the SIM card, not the mobile data. So it doesn't have the GPS or the data to tell me where they are. So I kept calling but they never answered. They just put their bag at the side and never bothered about it. It's a very old smartphone, but I disabled most of the apps*

already. The two girls are sharing one. Then in the end, at four o'clock plus, they finally reached home.

While she was certainly keen to avoid such situations, where the distress of not knowing her children's whereabouts was clearly unsettling, she was nevertheless resolute about controlling their mobile Internet usage. And although she had explored other options such, as GPS watches that offer location tracking, she was also practical about whether they would go down well with her children:

I'd rather have some GPS tracking. But if I give them the Internet just to track them, there are other consequences. They will be using it to play games. And kids at this age, they cannot control themselves. So I just don't give them mobile Internet access. I am still considering some GPS watches. And because the watch is not very fancy, it doesn't look good, they may not want to wear it.

Another reason for not adopting location-tracking services was because some respondents perceived Singapore as a generally safe country and they trusted the schools to keep their children safe:

Singapore is very safe, so I don't think I need a location-tracking app. My husband brings the child into the school, and my child will not run out from the school. The school will close the doors. I don't think it's necessary. I trust the school.—Jessie Loi, mother of one son aged 8

Nevertheless, some of our respondents, especially those with children in primary school, tended to welcome the school sending them digital notifications about their children's arrival to or departure from school. Such services would not involve the child personally updating the parent, yet could offer the assurance that such parents seek:

> *It will be good [to be notified by the school] when my children have reached or left school. I do not mind. You see we already have so many notifications every day, so if you mind, you can just close it, that will do. It's something that I can refer to.—Ho Pei Yi, mother of three daughters aged 6, 8, and 10*

None of the respondents reported the use of such a service by their children's schools. The closest thing to such a notification was the school attendance report that indicated whether a child was present or absent from school, and this record could be accessed via a phone app (see Figure 5.1 and 5.2).

Figures 5.1 and 5.2 School attendance report indicating whether a child is present or absent.

Interestingly, along with the emergence of apps such as Life360 that are targeted at parents of younger children, there is also a nascent market for apps that purportedly facilitate the physical safety of adults. The Companion app mentioned in the opening anecdote for this chapter allows users to invite family and friends from their phone contacts to track the user's whereabouts in real time and offers two special buttons. The self-explanatory "Call Police" button enables a swift one-touch action during emergency situations. The "I Feel Nervous" button allows users to inform their virtual companions when they feel unsafe. Virtual companions can also trigger an "Are you okay" notification on the user's phone, and if users do not respond within 15 seconds, their companions will be notified.

PARENTAL SURVEILLANCE ASSEMBLAGE

Besides ensuring their children's physical safety, another key concern of parents in Singapore is protecting their children from adverse peer influence. This concern was especially salient among parents with children in secondary school, who typically demand greater autonomy and independence and, indeed, are often granted it as well. In this regard, mobile-mediated connections are often enlisted by children to negotiate more independence from parental constraints, as previous studies such as Weisskirch (2009) and Caronia (2008) have also established. The following excerpt illustrates the typical parent-child arrangement. For Lisa Lin, a 39-year-old working mother, her daughter had just entered secondary school, and Lisa was considering whether she needed to give her child more personal freedom. It was precisely the contactability vested by the mobile phone that gave her more confidence to grant her daughter more autonomy:

> *I gave my girl a phone because it's easier to be contactable. Her school has a lot of activities, so the handphone is to protect her. At first, frankly speaking, I tried to install an app that can trace where she is. Later on, I gave up because I needed to pay a fee. [Back then] I asked her, "Once you get on the bus, call me. Reach school, call me. School hours end, call me." But now, I let go a bit. Now I only call to see how long it takes her to come back home. "Any issues, please call us." Because her lunch hour is at one p.m. plus, then the co-curricular activity starts at three-thirty p.m., so sometimes she calls me, "Mommy can I go with my friends to 7-Eleven or McDonald's or whatever." So I say, "Whenever you go out of school you must give me a call, then I will trust you, okay?" I trust her . . . I am just afraid that she will mix with the wrong group of people then behave badly or whatever. I just monitor her for a few months, then she should be okay. I make my girl call me so that I can hear her surroundings. When I was in school, my mom could not call me. I would go out on my own. So if it's time to release, you gotta release (laughs).*

Drawing on her own experience as a teenager, Lisa reasoned that allowing her child greater independence was part and parcel of growing up, and she wanted to give her daughter the freedom that she had enjoyed as an adolescent. By leveraging the contactability the phone connection afforded them, Lisa was thus granting her daughter a form of "monitored mobility" (Rutherford 2011, 81).

Complementing and augmenting these parent-child mobile contactability arrangements was a "parental surveillance assemblage" that comprised the mobile-connected networks of friends and classmates of children and networks of parents of the same. For Judy Lau, homemaker and mother to a 14-year-old secondary school boy and an 11-year-old primary school girl, she had to gradually ease her restrictions on her son:

> *Because he stays in school before the co-curricular activity starts, there are classmates who travel to the nearby shopping mall to have lunch. So actually the whole of last year, I told him, "You don't have to go with them, you just stay in school and have your lunch." I feel it's a bit unsafe, and because boys, they are a bit more immature. Then when they are out without adults, I think they will be up to no good. So I asked him, then he said, most of the time his friends would go out, then only he and a few boys would be alone in the canteen, and I think he can get along better with those who go out. [The kids] would even book Uber or Grab [taxi online], then go to the nearby mall. He said his friend would be willing to pay for the Uber or the Grab.*

Not wanting her son to feel left out and having the assurance of mobile contactability that enabled him to seek her permission when necessary, Judy relented over time:

> *Because I stay near the school and I also have friends who stay nearby, I told my son, "If you really want to go [anywhere], you'd better ask for [my] permission. If not, if you're going anywhere, you're gonna meet my friends, and they will tell me. Spies all around you!"*

Judy drew comfort from the fact that her network of friends in the neighborhood, well-connected to her via mobile phone, would be able to help keep an eye out for her son and alert her to any misbehavior. This threatened panoptic gaze was also likely raised and reiterated to instill self-discipline in her son, sensitizing him to the possible ramifications if he chose to disregard or disobey the rules she had set for him.

This parental surveillance assemblage, forged among groups of like-minded parents who shared similar concerns and priorities, connected and reinforced by the persistent mobile connections among all of them, proved crucial for several respondents. For Ivy

Loi, who was finding it increasingly difficult to discipline her 14-year-old son in secondary school, she managed to keep tabs on him even though she forbade him to have a phone:

> *If my son's friends' moms tell me about my son's behavior, it's good and bad. 'Cos I will be very angry. I just want him to be honest [to me rather than me relying on a location-tracking app]. He is getting naughtier. Once he was supposed to go home at this time. But he detoured to somewhere else. Unfortunately for him, my friend saw him. Then I asked him, "Where did you go just now?" He said, "Oh, at school." Then I said, "But my friend saw you at Junction 8 [a mall]. If you are coming home late, use your friends' handphone to call me, you have to. You made me worried." [I am] definitely okay with not being able to contact my son when he is apart from me, I've got his friends' numbers. I will call those boys [but] I try not to do that.*

Similarly, Esther Lee, a part-time tutor with three children aged 13, 11, and 5, explained how developing the network of contact numbers of her children's friends and their parents was both a crucial and valuable endeavor that she conscientiously undertook:

> *I always organize birthday parties for them, I get their friends' contacts, friends' parents' contacts. And then the next time if I see them going out with that friend, but if they are not back, I will know who to call. I also told them it was for safety reasons, "You need to tell me the name of one person and the contact number. I need to know the person. To have seen the person before."*

One thread running through the respondents' thoughts on surveillance over their children was their express need to insulate their children from adverse peer influence. Parents generally had reservations about their children engaging in unsupervised socializing, concerned that they would be led astray by peers who were bolder and had more permissive parents. They were deeply concerned that their children would not be able to resist deleterious peer influences and sought to restrict their opportunities for engaging too frequently in after-school socializing. Caronia (2008) cautions, however, that the perpetual contact mobile communication affords has enabled the creation of a new cultural model of "hyperparenting," with parents using mobile phones to exert more control over their children.

Fundamentally, a key issue underlying the use of mobile communication in parental protection of children is their impact on the quality of familial relationships. On this matter, some evidence is forthcoming from research on parents' use of mobile phone calls and texts to keep an eye on their children. Parental monitoring by mobile phone, while seemingly transactional, can adversely influence the quality of the parent-child relationship and levels of mutual understanding and trust. Weisskirch (2009) found that mobile phones can increase parental knowledge of their children's whereabouts and actions only when parent-child calls are initiated by the children rather than by parents. Notably, the study found that the more frequently parents call their children, the lower their levels of parental knowledge and the higher the levels of family disharmony. Similarly, Hasinoff (2017) also cautions that family-tracking apps, such as Life360, constrain children's autonomy and erode trust in the familial relationship. Building on these earlier studies and the findings presented in this chapter, it does emerge that there is a discernible parental inclination to harness a swathe of mobile communication devices and services to protect their children, but that such practices should be undertaken with caution. Arguably therefore, the growing incorporation of mobile communication into the parental surveillance assemblage can introduce tensions into the parent-child relationship that may not be healthy in the long run, particularly for the child's personal development.

SOCIAL MEDIA FOOTPRINTS

Beyond the adolescent years, parents may yet wish to exercise some measure of supervision over their children while recognizing that their children are more independent and need personal space and autonomy as they prepare for emerging adulthood. During that life stage, how do parents address this need to impose oversight? Enter social media, where young people share personal updates on their views and activities, and these become a veritable conduit for the parental gaze. Even if not explicitly designed for the purposes of surveillance, the dynamics of social media platforms, such as Instagram and Facebook, motivate users to post updates of their latest activities and locales. This has enabled parents of older teens and emerging adults to use their children's social media activities as a proxy for direct updates or notifications.

In research I conducted on Indonesian and Vietnamese university students in Singapore in 2014 (Lim and Pham 2016), we discovered that their parents would observe children's social media activities to find out how they were faring.

> *[My daughter] changed her Facebook profile picture. She already had a boyfriend, but that photo was with some other guy. I was upset. Maybe I am a very traditional woman. So I told her she should not post that photo because her boyfriend would be very sad. She told me, "You can't control me. My boyfriend was aware of that photo."—Mother of Lan, a female student in year 4, Business*
>
> *Actually, there were a few times that I went out with my friends and came home late and called my mother late. So my mother was irritated, like "Why do you hang out so late?" At that time, I was not very happy either . . . There was a day when she said, "When I did not see you do anything on Facebook, I was afraid you disappeared or went somewhere or something."—Nhung, a female student in year 2, Business*

Similarly, research I conducted on families with emerging adult children in Singapore (Lim and Lim 2015) had comparable findings. As one mother of university-aged children explained:

> *Sometimes I browse through their Facebook. They trust me and I trust them, I don't see why there will be privacy issues. If they consider me as [a] parent whom they turn to when they have problems, I don't see any privacy issue. I always must find out who are their friends and what's their activity with their friends. At least when they say they want to go out with their friends, I can imagine what kinds of activities they are doing.*

Again, studies in other parts of the world indicate that this trend is not peculiar to Asia. In her best-selling book *How to Raise an Adult* (2015), former dean of students at Stanford University Julie Lythcott-Haims shared how an American father was reassured that his daughter had arrived safely in London for her study abroad experience only when he saw her Facebook status update. Indeed, research on American students who attend residential colleges found that one key motivation for parent-child "friending" on social media platforms, such as Facebook, is to maintain familial connections in light of the physical distance between them (Yang 2018).

Fairly early on in the mobile phone revolution, several studies observed that these devices quickly morphed into the "electronic umbilical cord" that made it possible for American college students to remain in constant contact with their parents and to rely on them to help resolve daily problems (see Chen and Katz 2009; and Lee, Meszaros, and Colvin 2009). Notably, it was found that because college students contact their mothers to pour out their grievances and vent, such behavior may in turn encourage helicopter parenting behavior (Somers and Settle 2010). More recent research suggests that such mobile connections can strain the relationship because of the tussle between children wanting more autonomy and parents seeking more connectedness, thereby resulting in some instances of children engaging in avoidance behaviors, such as letting parents' calls go to voice mail (Kelly, Duran, and Miller-Ott 2017). Overall, mobile connectivity facilitates "stretching motherhood," as one study of mothers in New Zealand found (Longhurst 2013). Their mothering extends even to working adult children who have relocated to countries in different time zones, but who still maintain frequent contact via e-mail and/or Skype.

REFLECTION

This chapter has discussed how the proclivity toward close parental oversight and protectiveness over children has found, in mobile communication, a new platform for expression and assertion. Even as parents struggle to find the "right" amount of oversight to exercise, the proliferation of devices, apps, and services that enables parents to keep watch over their children seems only to grow. Indeed, a virtual industry has emerged to cater to these concerns. From webcams in the toddler years, to location-tracking apps and mobile devices in the tween years and beyond, mobile communication has enabled parents to maintain a strong presence in their children's lives throughout every life stage. Such apparatuses and services, and the techno-optimistic discourse surrounding them, constitute a veritable parenting assemblage (Deleuze and Guattari 1987). Parents can virtually keep their children company, or continue to cast a protective gaze over them, through this assortment of technological devices and services that helps extend the reach of parental oversight. These parents' virtually enabled omnipresence grants them a sense of reassurance that they are performing their parenting duties responsibly and responding to the acute sense of "risk consciousness" (Lee 2014) they have developed around their children's vulnerabilities.

Connected via a multitude of devices therefore, parents are kept in a perennial panoptic state where even after entrusting the child to another individual, they must seek to remain omnipresent via the use of these technological devices. This trend, coupled with the high premium placed on parents' protection and watchful supervision of their children in many Asian societies, has intensified the instinct to be digitally connected to one's child and accelerated the emergence of services that enable the same. The transcendent parent is thus both assured yet burdened by the constant mobile connections that link them to their children.

6

At Play

A mother waits for her teen son to go to bed before she peeks into his phone. The rule in the family is that he is to leave his phone in her room every night while it charges. She scans through the seemingly endless stream of WhatsApp messages he's exchanged with his friends and is struck by a conversation thread where the boys refer to a girl using vulgar and offensive terms. She makes a mental note to speak to her son about it, bracing herself for the drama that is sure to follow.

As children mature, they become independent social actors who manage their own peer interactions and relationships. While this is certainly a significant period of growth and identity exploration for young people, it can also be fraught with challenges and personal difficulties. Young people must tackle issues such as group norms, peer dynamics, and in-group and out-group fissures to best manage their relationships with friends and acquaintances. Aspects of social interaction such as peer pressure, loyalty, solidarity, and conflict will also come into play. Parents can perform a critical role in socializing their children, serving as sounding boards and helping them work through their differences with peers, while also inculcating them with positive values such as kindness and mutual respect. Young people's peer interactions are increasingly electronically mediated,

Transcendent Parenting. Sun Sun Lim, Oxford University Press (2020).

DOI: 10.1093/oso/9780190088989.001.0001

supercharged by their intense use of mobile media. Parents must artfully navigate both the online and offline environments in which their children interact to provide effective guidance, thus demanding transcendent parenting in the social realm as well.

Indeed, the process of peer interaction has become significantly richer but also more complex and demanding with the advent of mobile media. As young people increasingly have their own mobile devices that provide multiple pathways for them to connect directly to their peers, they have to manage their peer interactions in multifaceted ways (Lim 2013). Quite apart from the face-to-face interactions they will have with friends they meet in school or through other activities, such interactions will also trickle, nay, surge into the online, mobile-mediated space through apps such as Snapchat, Instagram, WhatsApp, and Facebook, each with its own set of features, communication norms, and relational cadences. The communication norms and rhythms forged in these apps both activate and complicate the relational patterns underlying young people's peer interactions. Notably, in the online realm, peer norms of mutual support and solidarity would involve a certain level of publicness and performativity as all interactions will be very visible to other members of their online social networks. How then does mobile communication alter the picture as parents seek to proactively guide their children in their social interactions with peers both online and off?

PEER INTERACTION

In their preschool years, children are largely under the care of their parents or appointed caregivers. Their social lives are planned and dictated by their parents, as is their access to digital devices and communication opportunities with others. However, the situation becomes decidedly more complex once children enter primary school and have the autonomy and maturity to engage in peer-to-peer interaction that is largely unsupervised by adults. This can happen on the fringes of classroom activity, during recess, on the school bus, and, increasingly, via online spaces. Notably, the ages at which children around the world are being given personal devices, principally mobile phones, is getting progressively younger. A survey in the United States found that in 2012 children typically received their first mobile phone between the ages of 10 and 12—by 2016, it had lowered to age 10 (Whitten 2016). Another study on fourth-year elementary school children in Australia found that in 2010 31% of the children owned or used a mobile phone, which then increased to 43% one year later (Howard 2017).

However, in both their face-to-face and online interactions, children need to understand the tacit rules of peer interaction. Over time, through trial and error, most young people will gradually understand how best to react and relate to peers in different contexts and situations to be sensitive to both their own needs and those of their peers. After all, socialization is a long and continuous process that involves a considerable degree of experience and experimentation, and children will find themselves in countless unstructured social situations over which they have very little knowledge and control. And yet, online peer interactions have characteristics that require more proactive socialization to fully prepare young people for the challenges they may encounter. Primarily, online peer interactions can be archived, are easily replicable, and highly public (boyd 2008). Given such characteristics, online peer interactions can be saved and stored, an individual's utterances can be copied and shared out of its original context, and these can all be disseminated to a large and indefinable audience. While not inherently problematic in and of themselves, these characteristics can be negatively exploited by cyberbullies to embarrass, tease, or shame victims; and the impact of such actions on young people can be severe, including negative emotions such as anger, sadness, frustration, embarrassment, stress, fright, loneliness, depression, or even self-harm and suicidal ideation (Slonje, Smith, and Frisén 2013).

Some respondents thus saw the need to vest in their children values that would stand them in good stead and go beyond the single-minded focus on academic achievement:

> *I hope that my children are responsible, not only academics-wise, but holistic-wise, their overall beings. It's important that they learn about life values and responsibility. It's not just study, study, study.—Judy Lau, mother of two children aged 11 and 14*

Many respondents thus deemed it important to be hands-on when guiding their children through ambiguous or awkward peer interactions to help them acquire a greater sense of perspective. For example, Esther Lee described herself as a counselor to her children in some typical circumstances:

> *Kids they will come back and tell you what happened in school, right? And their immediate reaction or response may not be the correct response, like, "I am angry at my friend because she did this." But you ask them, "What did she do? Why do you think you feel this way? Do you think she purposely meant to hurt you, or maybe she just did it unintentionally?" Yeah, so you guide them through the process, to let them know whether something should be taken personally, or if you can just act in a more appropriate way. 'Cos the kids, right, especially primary three, primary four students, they go through a stage where if there's something that they don't like, they will say, "I won't 'friend' you anymore!" It's very common. It happens usually with girls. Boys they play football, they fight, tomorrow they can still kick football together.—Esther Lee, mother of three children aged 5, 11, and 13*

As both the preceding and following quotes demonstrate, our respondents were also mindful of the different issues that were especially salient at specific stages of their children's development.

> *You know in these teenage years, they have a lot of crushes and what not. And I am in the Parent Support Group in the school, so I've heard a lot, I've seen a lot, so roughly we know what's happening in the school with the kids.—Joan Tan, mother of three children aged 7, 11, and 13*

Respondents with children in high school were especially concerned about their children engaging in romantic relationships with peers.

> *Actually I don't mind that Morgan [15 years old, secondary 3] has a girlfriend, but he must tell me. And one more important thing, he cannot touch [girls] because the consequences, he won't know. He understands. When he was in secondary one, I already told him, "You can have a girlfriend, female friend. You must let me know. I am not against such things." He doesn't want me to know because he feels that I am too naggy. I just worry that he may join the wrong groups. – Violet Cheung, mother of two sons aged 9 and 15*

MOBILE-MEDIATED PEER INTERACTION

In our current technological climate, the peer interaction issues that young people encounter at different developmental stages are also deeply intertwined with concerns surrounding their use of mobile communication and social media. As Rachel Simmons observed in her treatise on peer dynamics among American teenage girls: "It is now impossible to parent, teach, or even talk about girls without considering the roles of technology and social media in their lives" (2011, 104).

The adverse consequences of peer interactions that are mediated by mobile media were thus an often-mentioned parental anxiety. This stands to reason since on their mobile phones, children are independent agents who connect directly with their peers over multiple communication platforms. And these are increasingly multifaceted platforms that allow children to communicate directly with people whom they may know intimately from their own social circle, as well as strangers and online acquaintances whom they may not even have met in real life. Hence, our respondents were understandably concerned about the kinds of contact risks (Livingstone and Helsper 2008) their children would encounter, especially in light of active media coverage of such issues. As Samantha Sun, mother of three children, the eldest of whom was an 11-year-old boy, explained:

> *I read articles online. Other parents will share articles about things that happen to other kids: girls that are tricked into meeting men outside, kids that are bullied online, and they become depressed and kill themselves. We see a lot happening nowadays. Firstly, there are many predators online. My son plays Roblox. It's like a Lego-looking creature that is your avatar, and you work to build a house and earn money, and upgrade your house, and get a job. It is something like a reality game. You can play games and do different challenges to survive. So he showed me, "Mommy, this is my avatar." I told him, "There can be people who chat with you and say they are nine years old and go to the same school, [but they are really not]." So I warned him. I think social media [risks] are, firstly, predators, secondly, identity theft if you post a photo of your home and yourself. If people want to come and kidnap you, they have all your information. Thirdly, it is the pressure that my friends are all doing this, and they all live such perfect lives. You know, you only post the good things, so they have the*

> *wrong impressions. And then online bullying. So I think there are a lot of things for a child to handle, which we feel he is not ready for. We will [allow him more access to the Internet] when he is more mature.*

Managing their children's contact risks was thus something most of our respondents did on a regular basis, with some using apps to track their children's mediated interactions:

> *Actually this app [Safe Lagoon] duplicates his phone. Whatever that I see here is exactly what is in his phone. He's only active on WhatsApp. You need to know what the kids are up to. So they have the chat title right, "gathering" whatever. I just roughly browse through what are the chat groups' names. For some [chat groups' names] that are suspicious, I will click inside and see the chat [content].—Joan Tan, mother of three children aged 7, 11, and 13*

Besides the use of technological solutions, parents would also issue their children reminders to not befriend people whom they did not know from their face-to-face social circles, as well as imposing restrictions on social media accounts their children could be active on:

> *I told them they can only be friends [on social media] with people they know personally in real life. They might, they might not [do as I said]. I don't go down to that detail of checking every single person and asking them, "Who is this? Who is that?" because I will go mad doing that. But I am around, almost all the time. I keep them very involved and active. I don't let them arrange any outings with anybody that I don't know.—Esther Lee, mother of three children aged 5, 11, and 13*
>
> *When I started to be connected on Facebook with my children, I told them, "Don't accept any invites if you don't know who they*

> *are, you only accept invites if they are your classmates." For my daughter, she has a big group of friends, four or five of them. I know who she mixes around.—Lisa Lin, mother of two children aged 10 and 12*

Parents would also seek additional compliance by insisting that their children include them as "followers" or "friends" in their social media accounts. Even so, the children would find ways to circumvent or defy such conditions. Indeed, conflicts would occasionally erupt because parents and children simply could not see eye-to-eye on how readily they should allow parents into their social media circles, or how open they should be about letting their parents check the contents of their phones:

> *My son's friend's mom told me, "Your son is on Instagram." Ron [14 years old, secondary three] wouldn't tell me. [After we asked], he added his father in. But then he had two more accounts and blocked us. Even on WhatsApp, he's very naughty. He blocked me. I can't even see his photo. He would delete the WhatsApp messages after he read. I just said, "This is not right." He said, "For some of my friends, their parents do not read their WhatsApp. This is very rude." I said, "It's okay, because I want you to know that you need maturity."—Ivy Loi, mother of three children aged 8, 8, and 14*

As seen in the previous chapter on parental supervision, parents and children constantly negotiate the tensions between parents wanting to tighten the leash to exercise more protection and oversight, and children tugging away in a quest for greater independence. And yet, because our respondents are conscious of the challenges of mediated peer interactions, many erred on the side of caution and were quite upfront about their perceived need to directly pry into their children's online lives:

> *So I know Tim [13 years old, secondary one] has crushes. It's like an open secret, like, people will tease him, "Ooh, ooh, she's there, she's there." I kind of know that girl. I am very concerned about the chat between the girl and my boy. Because at this age, you can't stop them from having a relationship, but at the same time, we should discourage it because they are too young, you know, and studying comes first. In secondary one, they have a lot of things to cope with. But basically when I see the chat, they don't chat daily. Occasionally, "Hi, what are you doing?" "Do you miss me?" "Duh," yah, all these random chats. Nothing serious going on, I guess. That's why we need to monitor. We can't monitor all the chats, it's just too much to read. Sometimes in just one day they will have a few hundreds of chat messages. No time for that. So we can just randomly search.—Joan Tan, mother of three children aged 7, 11, and 13*

However, although parents may be motivated to address particular concerns they have about their children's mediated interactions, many of our respondents were also inclined to take a holistic view of their relationship with their children and recognized the value of granting the child some privacy and autonomy in the interest of boosting the long-term health of the parent-child bond. As Donald Winnicott observed, children will gradually come to develop and grow the "potential space" (1990; 2005), the tolerable distance they develop from their parents as they mature into individuals. Hence parents who instinctively grasped their children's need to cultivate this space tended to restrain themselves from directly interfering or becoming too involved in their children's mediated peer interactions so as not to alienate their children.

> *She [my daughter] got used to it already. I check her phone when she is around. "I check your handphone. Eh, give me your handphone." Midway she complained, "Why do you always look at my messages?*

> *You don't trust me!" So I said, "Nooo! Mommy just wants to know what's going on in your school. Is there any secret inside?" [She said], "No," [then I said], "Mommy also lets you look at my phone, right, and look at my messages!" She has Instagram, I leave it to her. She also has Facebook, but she did link us on Facebook. She doesn't [add me on Instagram] because I don't have an account. Sometimes I believe kids need freedom, some privacy also. I mean, we were kids before, we understand. So, I control you a bit, release you a bit. It's up to you whether you understand or not.—Lisa Lin, mother of two children aged 10 and 12*

Parents were slightly more interventionist when they perceived that their children could be led astray by their friends. The key concern many parents shared was that heightened contact with peers could make their children more vulnerable to destructive peer influence, ranging from the more mundane, such as exposure to profanities, or to more serious ones, such as pressure to conform to what parents deemed unhealthy group norms that spanned a range of contexts:

> *His friends sometimes write a lot of disgusting things that I don't think a child needs to know. They use all the vulgarities. I don't want my son to use them. I am very strict. Because he knows I will be reading, he won't dare. Sometimes I check my son's handphone, his friends send him videos and games to the class [WhatsApp] group chat, then I will scold him. I check his phone very strictly. When I see my son sending any message that is inappropriate, I will scold him, "Don't you think your friend can just screenshot and tell their mothers? Can you mind your language please?" He said I am the evil mum, I am very strict.—Ivy Loi, mother of three children aged 8, 8, and 14*
>
> *He said his friends are playing this game. In the game, they can buy credits, in-app purchases, and his friends also bought them. So I tell him I do not believe in using money for games, you play what is*

free, you are not going to use your money on these kinds of thing. So he suffers from peer pressure in that sense.—Samantha Sun, mother of three children aged 4, 6, and 11

I just told Crystal [13 years old, secondary 1] yesterday, "Why do you have to like all your friends' Instagram posts?" Then she told me it's a way of respecting them. Then I asked her, "But it doesn't really matter, why do you have to go and like them?" Because some of her friends actually count the likes and keep track of who likes their posts! Then I said, "They are too free!" Crystal spends some time on Instagram, and I don't like it. I said, "No, true friends will not go and count whether you like her posts or not, it's too picky."—Esther Lee, mother of three children aged 5, 11, and 13

As the experiences of these mothers reveal, peer influence pervades every realm of a young person's life, and parents have their work cut out for them in terms of keeping their children as firmly grounded as possible, even as the technological landscape throws up more challenges for young people. The publicness and replicability of mediated communication demands discretion, the competitive gaming environment tests restraint, and the performative nature of social media reinforces peer pressure.

PARENTAL INTERVENTIONS

"As communication becomes more impulsive, quick, and public, it also becomes coarser . . . What an adult grew up thinking belonged in a journal, or vented quietly to a friend, is today easily shared and commented on by multiple peers" (Simmons 2011, 108). In fact, many of our respondents were deeply cognizant of the very public nature of their children's mediated peer interactions. Particularly, as these mediated interactions are archived and transparent, clear for all to see, parents also leverage this affordance to proactively offer supervision and counseling, seizing specific opportunities to guide their children on how to best manage disputes and conflicts. However, as I will discuss later, transcendent parenting can be manifested in overactive parental interventions that may not be in the best interests of the children.

Let us first consider the experience of Geraldine Tay, a 46-year-old mother of four children. She was acutely conscious of the fact that her 15-year-old son Brandon was not socially adept due to his ADHD and that she had to be a constant guiding force. She had the practice of requiring her children to surrender their phones to her every night and would then scroll through their messages and social media feeds:

> *He loves to call people names, loves to joke. I always tell him, "A joke to you may not be a joke to other people." And these people who have ADHD don't have empathy, their EQ is quite low, so they don't really feel for other people. So I have to constantly counsel them. Sometimes, when things happen, I will look at his [social media] messages to see what happened. Yes, only yesterday I realized that he likes to take pictures of others to laugh at them. [I follow him on Instagram so] I know what he is doing, but I really don't know how to use Instagram. He likes to take people's unglam[orous] pictures. There are a lot of silly messages, unglam photos of other people [in his Instagram].*

Brandon's poor social awareness motivated Geraldine to review his social media feed so that she could detect any inappropriate or unwelcome behavior and advise him on the preferable response or course of action in different circumstances. Whereas she would not be privy to his face-to-face interactions with his peers and would be unable to observe or advise on whether his conduct was appropriate, she could do so in the online setting. She was able to remind him that his act of taking less than attractive pictures of his peers and posting them on Instagram would not go down well.

On a separate occasion, Geraldine also discovered that her son was making fun of his teacher in the WhatsApp group chat and had to personally intervene.

> *For example, he was calling the teacher names among the whole chat group. I can't recall [what it was], [it was] some funny name which I found very rude. My son started calling the teacher names because he had misunderstood my son. So it's like that. If you misunderstand my son and accuse him of something he never did, he will really do anything for revenge. Yeah, I had to tell my son, "Even though the teacher may have scolded you wrongly, you cannot say things like that in front of everybody. [That would be] so bad. You can tell the teacher at the side and say, 'Actually this is what happened and I'm not at fault.'" So what I did is [I made my son] apologize to [the teacher]. Meanwhile, I had to call the teacher and explain to him.*

In this instance, one could say the mother's effort to mediate the awkward state of affairs was propitious, if not crucial, for her son's well-being. Since by her assessment he lacked the social awareness to appreciate that his outburst and open name-calling of his teacher within the very public group chat was highly improper, her intervention was critical. By encouraging him to express his contrition in a public fashion, while also reaching out personally to mend fences with his teacher, she could both counsel her son and help restore his relationship with his teacher.

However, it is difficult to say if parental interventions in such matters are always desirable or helpful. The situation can get unnecessarily dicey and complicated when there are conflicts among peers, and parents then intervene and take sides, even advocating for their children:

> *Previously in primary six, one of Crystal's friends had committed to going to a chalet [sleepover]. At the last minute she pulled out and refused to give an explanation. Crystal was quite angry. In the group chat, she said, "I hate you. You are always pulling out of things. This is not nice at all. When you are committed to something, you must follow through." Exclamation marks, exclamation marks, blah, blah, blah. This girl was known to have this habit. At the last minute, she pulls out. So it's not that particular incident, it's an accumulation of incidents. The girl's mum is a teacher who was also in the chat group. She took print screens and went to inform the school's teacher that Crystal should be subjected to disciplinary action. But I refused to let that happen. I spoke to the teacher. Crystal later said, "I am sorry for using the exclamation marks. I was really angry." I think her anger was justified. So I explained to the disciplinary teacher, the form teacher, showed them the messages. I had actually deleted the messages, but there were other friends who kept the messages and took print screens and sent them over. So, Crystal apologized and her anger was justified, and she didn't use vulgarities. The teachers agreed that this is okay. The mom should not have involved the school. The mom didn't tell the school the whole picture. Then I told Crystal, "Learn this lesson well. You never know when people will take print screens."—Esther Lee, mother of three children aged 5, 11, and 13*

In this situation involving two 12-year-old girls, their two mothers became deeply enmeshed in the conflict as a consequence of the very public nature of their altercation. The patently viewable and visible exchange between the two girls provided fodder for their mothers to "forensically" unpack the conflict, analyze and compare how justifiable each girl's behavior was, and to openly lobby for their children vis-à-vis their teachers. What was otherwise a typical quarrel between two schoolgirls, which may well have blown over with time, was allowed to escalate to the point that disciplinary action was imposed by the school and then successfully averted through parental intervention. Crystal's mother was also aided by her friends who had saved the messages, thereby extending involvement in this conflict well beyond the two families. In the absence of such compelling documentary evidence, further enabled and fortified by underpinning networked interactions, it is doubtful whether the extent of parental involvement would have been as great. It is interesting to note that Crystal's mother took the opportunity to caution her daughter about the possibility of "print screens" being taken in such situations and to take that lesson to heart. As this account also reveals therefore, parents must now go beyond offering advice about handling peer dynamics to also providing guidance on the complexities of networked peer interactions and the self-protection strategies one must exercise online.

More crucially, accounts such as this indicate that with mobile communication intensifying, and more of such mobile-facilitated and mobile-accelerated communication patterns rising to the fore, the situation of context collapse (Wesch 2009) has been superseded by what I will call context merge. Michael Wesch observed that social media platforms heralded the situation where the divisions between people in disparate contexts of an individual's life erode, such that the self that one presents in one context, for example family, is now visible to those who are accustomed to seeing the individual in another context, such as their professional lives. He argues that this can lead to discomfiting situations where people not used to seeing the individual in a particular context can now do so freely. In the case of these children and parent WhatsApp groups, the two contexts of child-child interaction and parent-parent interaction are now virtually fused through mobile connections. With some children using their parents' phones for these group interactions, and parents checking these group messages on their children's phones, parents and children are now huddled together into one tight online space, interacting rather intensively in a manner that was not previously possible. As one mother who is a parent-leader in the school laments, the lack of boundaries in these groups poses distinct challenges for setting desirable norms for both parents' and children's participation in them:

> *I want to build an environment where we are very supportive parents' groups, really on the positive side, and not continue to berate or make all the negative comments, which actually is not so good for the whole class. Actually my children do read all the WhatsApp messages. They would use my phone to read. I welcome them to read them because sometimes there are parents who call out for help, or ask for notes or homework, and I will just tell them to share whatever you have. There were some bullying cases in the past, I also told the class to stop speculating. Put a stop to all these [negative] comments. Some mummies in the group came to me and said that they appreciated that I stepped out and told these parents to stop making all these comments. Children need a lot of support. And if my children are reading the group chat, they are seeing the parents as examples in daily life, in society. We do not want them to make speculations.—Sophie Chua, mother of two children aged 10 and 11*

However, it is unrealistic to expect parents to always behave in a manner that is mature and helps promote the most positive environment for online peer interactions.

> *For WhatsApp, sometimes I don't like this disrespectful [atmosphere]. Because [my son's] class has an autistic boy. During primary one and two, the boy was in the same class as him. The boy kept picking or hitting other children, because he has a medical condition. So the other parents were not aware of it. But I happened to be aware of it. And the parents of the autistic boy just didn't want to be*

in the WhatsApp group. I think they knew that there would be a lot of complaints. Some parents said things like, "Oh, my girl got hit in the eyes," "My boy got pushed today by B." If the boy's parents were in the WhatsApp group, how would they feel? They would feel like, "Oh, I am so embarrassed," "I feel disrespected because you are discussing my boy among yourselves." I think they will be very offended by the messages. But there's no right or wrong because the boy did hit the other children. I think the WhatsApp also creates a strained relationship or friendship among parents. Sometimes when they discussed the autistic boy, I just didn't want to be involved in the discussion. I didn't reply to them. I felt so disgusted by their words. Maybe [the words were even] unkind. It's the way they phrased it. I understand that as parents, when their children get hit, maybe they get anxious. But maybe they should take it directly to the teacher instead of discussing here [over WhatsApp]. It shows a bad side of the boy. Other parents will know. More people will know, "Oh, THIS boy."—Jenna Chang, mother of two children aged 6 and 9

Parents may not be conscious of, or even choose to willfully disregard, the norms and mores that should underpin the creation of a civilized atmosphere within the social media groups that emerge around their children's school lives. As the following account will demonstrate, the connectivity among parents complicated the children's face-to-face social interactions:

There were a few incidents where my kids were being bullied. But later we found out that the boy actually had leukemia, so he could not go to kindergarten, and he missed out on a lot of education on social behavior. I brought up the example and shared with the group that even if the person can be a bully, it could be because of certain reasons. So go to the teacher, let the teacher know, instead of going to the students, telling the students off. There was one incident where

> *there was some misunderstanding in the class and a student was hurt. But the parents of another student who was not involved in the incident started complaining in the group chat, "Oh, if my girl were hit by the boy like that, I will surely sue and complain all the way to the Ministry of Education." And then another person went in and supported the idea. So the comments were added on, like what you see on the Internet. As a facilitator I had to step in and ask them to stop speculating on what happened because this incident happened in class. Leave it to the parents who were involved to discuss offline. And the funny thing is I asked my son what happened, and, he said, "Oh, so and so hit somebody with a book, but I think it was an accident, I don't know." And because the culprit involved in the incident was one of my friends' child, I texted her and said, "Eh, do you know your son is involved in this issue, can you go and check it out? Did he tell you what happened?" Then she said, "Oh, no I didn't even know they were talking about my son."—Sophie Chua, mother of two children aged 10 and 11*

As with the experience of Crystal above, WhatsApp interactions among parents about squabbles between children can escalate quickly, with alliances being formed within the group and people taking sides and pledging allegiances. It also complicates the task for teachers who will eventually be required to mediate the conflict since it had occurred within the school.

Indeed, the ease of mobile communication and the culture of constant connectivity between parents and teachers that has been forged do seem to pave the way for a more intense level of parental involvement in the children's social interactions within school than has been previously witnessed, as demonstrated in this e-mail from a father to a teacher about his son's scuffle with classmates in school:

Email title: Punch up in school field
Date: 30 August, 2017, 20:44
Dear Mdm XXX,
Apologies to inconvenience you during this holiday period.
Max told me he was involved in a punch up over a misunderstanding during football at recess. Details as follows:
Date: 30 Aug 2017
Est time of incident: 10:10 (recess time)
Location: School field

Max and some classmates went to the school field to play football. At some point during the game, a free kick was given to the team opposing Max. Unknowingly, Max mistakenly kicked the ball.

Jack Tan and Daryl Pang (who were supposed to take the free kick) probably mistook Max's actions and started to punch his stomach and upper body. Max fell over and ended up on the floor, stunned by the incident.

At this point, it is not known if other people witnessed this incident.

Matthew Seah on the opposite side of the field noticed Max lying on the field ran to help him up. After that, everyone continued playing football.

Max did not inform anyone about this until I found out about it after work. There are faint red marks with the most serious, a small bruise on his upper left arm (photo attached). He has not complained of stomach pain but I will continue to monitor his situation. We do not need to seek medical advice at this moment.

The level of detail with which this father reported the scuffle to the teacher in order to champion his son's innocence is remarkable. Titled "Punch up in school field," the e-mail vividly recounts the chain of events and is illustrated with photographs of his son's injuries that were most likely taken with a smartphone. The compelling nature by which this appeal was lodged, complete with photographic evidence, reflects how the ease and intensity of mobile communication have helped draw parents ever-more profoundly into the lives of their children. In the prevailing mobile phone culture that we increasingly take for granted, with ever-present, multifunctional mobile devices that enable us to engage in rich, multimodal and instantaneous connections, the protective instinct for parents to document and act on such incidents is perhaps stronger than ever. It is in precisely such a mobile-media-infused landscape that parents can and *do* engage in transcendent parenting.

Strikingly, parents would exploit multiple mobile affordances, including social media, to gather intelligence about school-related incidents as captured in Figure 6.1. While this is fundamentally within their right, it is perhaps also symptomatic of the high level of parental involvement in their children's lives. In so doing, they may deny their children the latitude to acquire greater autonomy and engage in independent problem-solving:

> *There was a time the hawker in school was quite rude to my daughter. He shortchanged her when she bought something. When she asked for [the correct] change: "Uncle, how come you still haven't given me twenty cents?" Then he said, "No need to care lah, never mind, go" in a rude way. She came back and cried, saying, "Uncle is very rude." So I posted on the Facebook group, asked if other people had these kinds of cases. There were people who said yes . . . When I posted there, I hoped that the parent support group in charge should be able to talk to the hawkers. See, there are thirty comments [after I posted].*

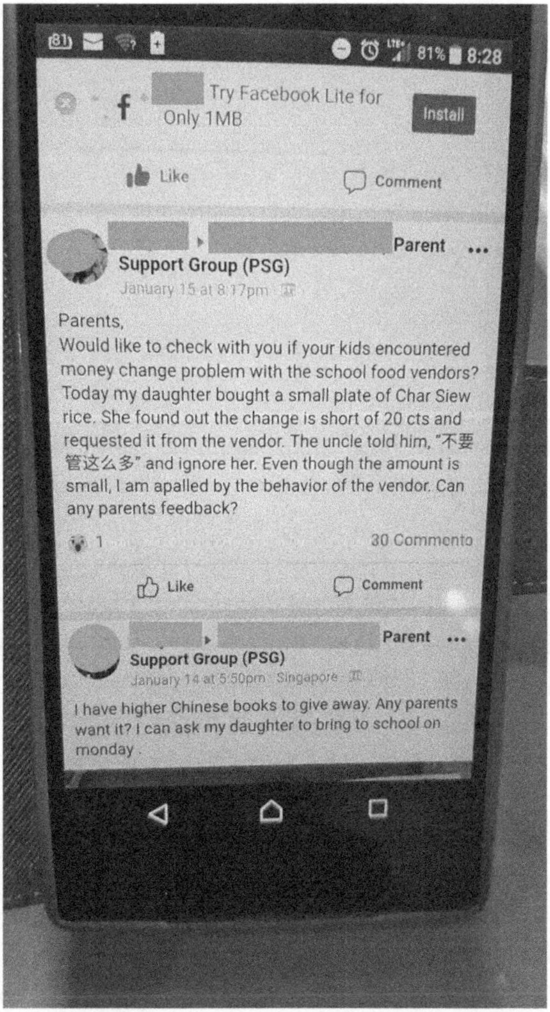

Figure 6.1 Low Ting Ting's Facebook post in her daughter's school parent support group.

There are other incidents [posted after me] as well. I just want to keep a record there. When there's anything happening, I can go and keep track.—Low Ting Ting, mother of two daughters aged 8 and 10

Ultimately, it remains to be seen whether parental intervention in such piddling matters benefits anyone and whether it creates an unsavory culture of parental interference.

REFLECTION

As I have discussed in this chapter, parents can become (too) heavily involved in their children's peer interactions, both online and offline, especially since they are so concerned with the children's "contact risks" (Livingstone and Helsper 2008). With online interactions leaving a visible digital trail, parents can and *do* engage in transcendent parenting, seeking to openly or furtively gain insights into their children's social media conversations to spot potential issues and offer guidance. In some sense, this offers an unprecedented opportunity for parents to better understand their children, to observe how they behave in mediated social situations with their peers, and to provide valuable guidance. However, these are ultimately intrusions that may affect the parent-child relationship and the degree of mutual trust they forge. The extent to which the child's privacy is compromised is also open to debate.

At the same time, parents who then choose to act on the intelligence they gather from records of their children's social media activity may also run the risk of becoming overly involved, depriving their children the opportunity to exercise autonomy and develop problem-solving skills. As danah boyd argued from her study of American teens' use of MySpace, social network sites enable young people to "work out identity and status, make sense of cultural cues, and negotiate public life" (2008, 120). Observing the dynamics of mutual interactions, validations, and admonishments of peers in socially media are precious opportunities for learning to interpret social situations and to manage their online and offline personae.

Arguably, this inclination to be drawn into their children's affairs is also reflective of the strong instinct among Asian parents to protect their children as discussed in Chapter 5. Indeed, the situation becomes potentially more fractious and complicated when parents and children are subjected to the context merge I described earlier, that is, being able to interact across previously existing barriers. Disputes among children then extend to the adult space with parents actively advocating for their children and lines of allegiance among different parents erupting in some situations. However, such active interference may severely undermine their children's abilities to nurture a healthy "potential space" from their parents as they develop, robbing them of an essential maturation experience. Young people who have to resort to adult intervention to mediate peer and sibling disputes are thus less experienced with managing and resolving these conflicts on their own—a valuable learning opportunity (Rutherford 2011). As it is, young people are already restricted in the freedom they enjoy from parents since they rely on them for financial support (Holloway and Valentine 2000). However, transcendent parenting may amplify young people's dependence on their parents for emotional support and further constrict spaces for personal growth. At the same time, the ability of parents to constantly assert their presence in their children's personal social lives through transcendent parenting, even if well-intentioned, adds yet another hefty task to the parenting burden.

7

Mobile Communication and Transcendent Parenting

She crawled gratefully into bed after a hectic day at the conference she was attending in Montreal. She was worn out from jet lag due to the 12-hour time difference with Singapore. She slept soundly before being rudely awakened by the persistent ringing of her phone. "It's 2 a.m.! Who could be calling me at this hour?" she thought, silently cursing that she'd forgotten to turn it off because she was too exhausted. "Mrs. Tan? This is Mrs. Prakash, the science teacher! Your son needs the new workbook for term two. It was sold out last term but has just been reissued. And the school bookshop has run out. Can you get it from other bookshops? He's been missing it for the last two lessons. Thanks for your support. He really needs the book! Okay?" *Before Mrs. Tan could even reply, the teacher rang off. Mrs. Tan looked at her phone, bewildered. She realized miserably that because it was 2 p.m. in Singapore, her son's school day had just ended and even though she was miles from home, she now needed to track down a bookshop to buy that elusive workbook.*

Transcendent Parenting. Sun Sun Lim, Oxford University Press (2020).

DOI: 10.1093/oso/9780190088989.001.0001

That mother was me.[1] I realized then that no matter how far I am from my children, that I have to parent them, constantly. And that the mobile phone is a key instigator of this enduring and unyielding tie between us. Reachable at all times by my children, contactable always by their teachers and classmates' parents, my trusty iPhone with its shiny surface and colorful apps binds me, inexorably, to my duties as a parent. As a working mother, I treasure the liberty and flexibility my phone brings me. I can still manage office matters even when nursing my sick child at home or while awaiting my turn at parent-teacher meetings. And nothing beats a cheerful Snapchat greeting from my kids when I am away on a business trip. Yet I can't help but feel the occasional jolt of resentment at how relentlessly the phone reminds me of my parenting obligations. WhatsApp messages from other parents, calls from teachers, and pings from the ClassDojo app punctuate my day, wherever I or my beloved children may be.

Is my story unique? Hardly, as the experiences of my respondents in the preceding pages have revealed. The mobile communication era has ushered in the practice of transcendent parenting, enabled and intensified by the proliferation of apps, channels, and platforms that link parents to their children and the key institutions in their lives. Indeed, throughout every stage of their children's development, from infancy to adolescence to emerging adulthood, the mobile-enabled parent can and does transcend every realm of their children's lives. They transcend the physical distance between them and their children, their children's offline and online social interaction spaces, as well as the "timeless time" that seems to make parenting duties ceaseless and relentless.

1. It is perhaps a reflection of Singapore's patriarchal society and the role of women as mothers that my children's primary school teachers almost always referred to me by my married name "Mrs Tan" rather than address me as "Ms Lim."

Powered by smartphones that virtually accompany families through all aspects of their everyday existence, at work, at play, or at rest, these mobile connections both embody and convey the many priorities parents deem central to their lives. Paramount among these would be the safety, well-being, and positive development of their children. As I have argued throughout this book, transcendent parenting is deeply imbricated with the goals that guide parents as they raise their children, and the trials they must overcome throughout this journey.

TRANSCENDENT PARENTING ACROSS DIFFERENT REALMS

Mobile communication was a unifying thread running through the gamut of activities, both mundane and momentous, in the daily throb of these families' lives. As you have seen in the course of this book, parents spoke with resolute determination about their best efforts to groom their children into capable, successful individuals who could fend for themselves in the future. And ensuring that their children excelled academically formed the cornerstone of this parenting endeavor.

As they sought to nurture their children, managing the daily grind of schoolbags, homework, spelling tests, and reminders from teachers, lofty academic aspirations underscored their parenting labors. And mobile communication served as the indispensable ally of these parents, helping them ensure that all assignments were accounted for, school announcements noted, and meetings with teachers dutifully attended. We therefore saw in Chapter 3, "At Home," the strong sense of responsibility parents felt toward their children and how they actively incorporated mobile media into their lives to micro-coordinate and lubricate the family's daily routines in the best interests of their children. Their desire to construct a healthy media environment for their children was also notable. Indeed, the trope of parental determinism (Furedi 2002) loomed large, heightened by long-held Asian conceptions of parental obligations to support their children in the quest for academic excellence (Chao 1995; Chen and Luster 2002). Working parents in particular would harness mobile media to transcend their professional and family lives to manage their duties on both fronts.

As we entered the realm of education in Chapter 4, "At School," the distinct and sizeable roles that mobile communication plays in parenting duties became even more pronounced. The active mobilization of home-school conferencing apps, parent-parent chat groups, gradebooks, and homework helper apps underlined just how critical these services are for parents who wish to be actively engaged with their children's school lives. We saw how the ever-multiplying channels by which parents can communicate with their children's teachers and other parents, along with platforms that directly involve parents in their children's learning, intensify transcendent parenting practices. Parents diligently managed, albeit sometimes grudgingly, the relentless notifications from these apps and chat groups to keep their children on track in school, with working parents keeping tabs even from their workplaces. Such affordances, even if deemed beneficial, seemed only to exacerbate the parenting time famine (Furedi 2008). Indeed, some parents admitted to feeling as though they were in school with their children and to an especially acute sense of pressure when the children's examinations were in progress. Some also contrasted this higher level of parental involvement with their own parents' relatively lighter burdens when they were themselves in school. In essence, mobile-enabled parents parent constantly, transcending the home, school, and workplace environments via these communication linkages that bind them inextricably to their children. By some accounts, with peer comparisons and peer pressure being galvanized in public platforms such as WhatsApp group chats, the competitiveness of the educational race also seems to be stiffer and more palpable than ever before.

Transcendent parenting practices extend also to the parental urge to protect children from physical harm and online risks, drawing again on the increasingly sophisticated affordances of mobile communication. As we saw in Chapter 5, "Out and About," parental protectiveness and oversight has found a new lease of life in webcams and CCTV cameras, location-tracking devices and services, mobile phone connections, and social media footprint. A virtual industry of such technologies has flourished, enabling parents to transcend the physical distances between them and their children in order to feel assured of their safety, however illusory that feeling may be. Indeed, such apparatuses and services, as well as the mobile-connected social networks of these families, constitute a veritable parenting assemblage (Deleuze and Guattari 1987) that casts a protective eye over the children. Even when their children are not by their side, parents can—and some try hard to—extend the reach of their oversight. At the same time though, this assemblage does keep parents in a perennial panoptic state, so that they remain omnipresent in their children's lives via these technological devices. Given the valorization of parental control and supervision in Asian society, the perceived need and desire to be digitally connected to one's child have thus encouraged transcendent parenting practices.

Beyond merely exercising oversight, parents also feel duty bound to socialize their children, guiding them through the ups and downs of their peer interactions, both online and offline, as well as managing their contact risks (Livingstone and Helsper 2008). In this regard, Chapter 6, "At Play," discussed how online interactions leave a visible digital trail, allowing parents to openly or furtively gain insights from their children's social media conversations with their peers to identify potential issues and offer advice. Such digital footprint provides parents an unprecedented vantage point from which to observe how their children behave in mediated social situations, so as to better guide them. On a more complex plane, I also discussed in Chapter 6 the awkward situation of "context merge" where parents and children can interact across previously existing barriers through messaging app chat groups. Almost like a playground scuffle between children that erupts into a fight among their respective parents and other parties who bear witness and take sides, this situation of context merge allows disagreements between children to seep into the adult space and can prove divisive for overall group dynamics. Another interesting facet of transcendent parenting was also seen in Chapter 6 in the form of parents' strategic use of mobile communication to involve and insert themselves into their children's offline peer interactions. We saw how parents leveraged the multimedia affordances of mobile communication to convey to the teacher their children's grievances pertaining to an altercation in school, furnishing even photographs and incident reports to seek justice on their children's behalf. Taken together, all these practices exemplify the growing use of mobile media by parents to transcend their children's online and offline peer interactions, to exert greater involvement, and provide more active guidance. This is yet another manifestation of transcendent parenting and the new responsibilities it can constitute.

I must also highlight that, ultimately, transcendent parenting is platform- and device-agnostic. Enabled and invigorated by always on, always available mobile media, transcendent parenting is not especially acute for users of any particular devices or platforms. Regardless of whether parents and children are linked by smartphones, feature phones, tablets, laptops, or mobility trackers, irrespective of whether the family communicates via WhatsApp, Facebook Messenger, Snapchat, LINE, or plain old SMS, the very state of electronically mediated connectedness creates the possibility and therefore the turn toward transcendent parenting. While all devices and platforms come with their own affordances, rhythms, forms, and norms of communication, they nevertheless plug into an all-encompassing connective web binding parents to their children in a digitalized cloud of affection, care, duty, and reciprocity.

TRANSCENDENT PARENTING OR TRANSCENDENT MOTHERING?

Throughout the book, it does appear as though mothers assume the lion's, or rather the lioness', share of parenting duties, especially those pertaining to the child's academic performance. While this certainly does reflect the prevailing situation in many countries, there are some encouraging signs that the parenting partnership is evolving in different parts of the world, albeit at varying speeds. Prior research has found that although mothers in Western societies are still responsible for most physical childcare duties, it seems that within intact families, fathers' family involvement is growing both in absolute terms and in comparison to mothers' involvement (Pleck 2010; Goldscheider, Bernhardt, and Lappegård 2014; Yeung 2016). Yet more recent research suggests that the stress mothers experience in balancing the obligations of work and home is only getting more acute. Collins (2019) concludes from her interviews with mothers in Germany, Italy, Sweden, and the United States that far from attaining work-life balance, these women must tackle work-life conflict. They suffer from the pressures of unrealistic expectations of mothers that are neither buttressed by concrete structural changes nor policy interventions.

The picture in Asia is also not particularly sanguine, although there may be some room for hope. Time-use data indicates that even though the participation of Asian men and women in the labor market is equally high, Asian fathers have a lower level of family involvement compared to their Western counterparts (Tsuya and Bumpass 2004; Yeung 2016). This may be due to sociocultural norms that have persisted over time, such as in Vietnam where traditional gender divisions have become ingrained, or structural factors, such as in Japan where men tend to have longer working hours (Yeung 2013). Yet the prospect of gender parity in parenting within Asian households is not entirely bleak as cultural beliefs and societal priorities can influence behavior. For example, Hindu fathers in India believe that performing parenting duties will earn them salvation and thus discipline and guide their children, while in Shanghai, fathers are known to help their children with homework and take them to enrichment classes due to the valorization of academic achievement (Yeung 2013).

Notwithstanding the above, even if the transition toward a more gender-equal distribution of the parenting burden is not imminently realizable, I have steadfastly resisted the urge to refer to this phenomenon as transcendent mothering. Principally, my concerted decision to use "transcendent *parenting*" encompasses an aspirational dimension that aims to capture the more desired and, indeed, more desirable state of shared parenting responsibilities. In societies where dual-income households are becoming increasingly common, it no longer makes sense to privilege the mother's parenting obligation, and more structures must be put in place to ensure that fathers shoulder a more equitable share of parenting responsibilities. Essentially however, given the critical role that mobile media play in the lives of families, I believe that transcendent parenting is already being experienced by both parents, even if to unequal degrees. As conceptions of the parenting duties that fathers and mothers should bear evolve, the experience and practice of transcendent parenting will alter as well.

THE UNIVERSALIZING EXPERIENCE OF TRANSCENDENT PARENTING

Throughout the book, I have mostly focused on the transcendent parenting practices of parents in Singapore. To what extent then can the Singapore experience be extrapolated to the rest of Asia's urban middle class and beyond? Indeed, parenting is in many ways a universalizing experience, through which the middle class around the world are bound together by "a host of context-specific desires, aspirations, and anxieties" (Heiman, Liechty, and Freeman 2012, 20). More specifically, as I discussed in Chapter 2, "Parenting Today," common threads do run through Asia in terms of three main parenting priorities that preoccupy the urban middle class: inculcating values in their children to ensure positive maturation, exercising oversight and supervision to protect them from harm and adverse influence, and providing support for their children's academic achievement to pave their way for future success.

Notably Asian parents' sense of duty toward monitoring their children's whereabouts, behavior, and peer interactions is evinced by the growing use of mobile technologies for surveillance and location tracking. CCTV cameras and webcams are increasingly being introduced in institutional settings such as preschools. In Malaysia for example, the government supported the development of the MyMata (literally "my eye" in Malay) surveillance system for use in one government nursery to "enhance the safety and security of children" (Chung 2016). The videos are stored in a cloud server for up to a month and parents can view them on their mobile phones and laptops, with the plan to introduce the MyMata system in nurseries across Malaysia. Similarly, in Vietnam's financial capital Ho Chi Minh City, the proportion of nursery schools and kindergartens with CCTVs installed is high (48% for public nursery schools, 73% for private nursery schools, 53% for private kindergartens) (Tuoi

Tre Online 2018). A survey conducted by Ho Chi Minh City's Department of Education and Training found that a sizeable 88% of Vietnamese parents expressed approval for installing CCTVs in their preschoolers' classrooms, but only 48% of Vietnamese teachers felt likewise as they perceived such CCTVs as a privacy intrusion (Tuoi Tre Online 2018). These trends parallel those we see in Singapore as discussed in Chapter 5, "Out and About." Arguably, such instances also reflect more broadly the mutual interaction of underlying values and contemporaneous trends within Asia's urban middle class—the rising availability and use of communication technologies and the growing acceptance of the (albeit debatable) benefits of surveillance, coupled with intense parental investment in children.

With regard to academic pursuits, the concern for academic success seems more pronounced than ever among Asia's urban middle class in economically vibrant cities in countries such as China, Indonesia, Malaysia, South Korea, and Vietnam. Parents' avid push for their children's educational achievement is reflected in the flourishing markets for tuition and enrichment classes (Bray and Lykins 2012). At the same time, schools in these cities are also adopting a broad swathe of mobile communication services for home-school conferencing and online learning, with parents reportedly discomfited by their effects. In India, an ever-growing number of schools are implementing locally developed apps, such as Teno, that facilitate home-school conferencing in view of the positive response from parents (EdTechReview 2016). In China, the trend toward technology use in home-school conferencing is particularly aggressive. For example, the city of Chongqing in China has mandated that all educational institutions from kindergarten through middle school set up official WeChat accounts to facilitate teachers' communication with parents and students. However, the uses of WeChat by teachers go well beyond sending announcements and reminders to become a veritable extension of the classroom (Sun 2016). Teachers use to it monitor and review students' homework submissions before subsequently phoning the children to remind them to submit their corrections by midnight. Concurrently, the app will send these notifications to parents to secure their support in supervising the child's timely completion of assignments. These Chinese parents are reportedly so stressed by the relentless homework reminders on their phones that they have resorted to silencing them, echoing the experiences of some Singapore parents as discussed in Chapter 4, "At School."

Another notable example is the Home-School Communication System (*Xiaoxuntong*), which is widely used in schools across China's Guangdong Province (Cheng 2015). Alarmingly, peer pressure for students is heightened through this system because teachers use mass messages to publicly call out specific students' bad behavior and to highlight examples of students with strong academic performance: "Xiao Mui improved a lot in the Maths exam; while Xiao Tian and Xiao Ming received a fail grade" (Cheng 2015, 122). Such features and practices create extreme pressure on parents and students alike to engage in social comparison and serve to significantly amplify the school's unhealthy and competitive environment (Cheng 2015). As harsh as such public shaming may appear to readers in the West, social norms in China condone such public shaming of children, as children must fulfill obligations to the family, principally through excelling in school and gaining face for the family (Chao and Tseng 2005). Such accounts certainly highlight the extremes to which these home-school conferencing systems and the imprudent uses to which they are put can have unwelcome effects on the very stakeholders they are meant to serve. Ultimately, we must also ask in whose interests home-school conferencing is ultimately undertaken—those of parents or of children, and if so, how can the rights and needs of children be more respectfully honored?

Parent-parent communication via apps such as WeChat has also served to heighten peer pressure and rivalry among parents. The convenience and immediacy of communication via platforms such as WeChat have fostered an environment that is both self-indulgent and self-aggrandizing. Parents openly flaunt their children's achievements on these platforms and ingratiate themselves to teachers to earn preferential treatment. For example, instead of sending a private message to a teacher to express appreciation for her tutelage, a parent may send a message to the entire group of parents and the teacher to publicly praise her for helping the child win a competition. In doing so, the parent forges positive social capital with the teacher, while glorifying the child's triumph, although likely earning the ire and resentment of other parents. These chat groups have also been used (and abused) for sharing inspirational messages, product advertisements, and even virtual red envelopes containing digital money. These controversial applications of chat groups have not gone unnoticed by the Chinese authorities who have since sought to prescribe guidelines prohibiting commercial uses and the public sharing of students' academic results (Cheng 2015). While efforts by Chinese parents to sharpen their children's "competitive edge" through gifts for teachers are not new, the publicness of such chat groups has distinctly raised the stakes for parent-teacher communication and made the performative dimension of parenting significantly much more pronounced. Similar trends have also been noted in India where parents take to social media to brandish the achievements of their students, such as posting pictures of their children's report cards when they attain high scores, thus creating a culture of "relentless comparison" (Bandyopadhyay 2017). In Vietnam, the propensity among parents to share photos of their children and trumpet their academic triumphs via social media reached such extremes that from June 2017, to protect the privacy of children aged seven and above, a new Law on Children made it illegal for parents to post their children's private information online (including their identification details, school reports, and even networks of friends) without the children's consent (Vietnamnet 2017).

In sum, the resonance across the experiences of these disparate Asian countries, with those of Singapore parents that I have shared earlier in the book, suggests that transcendent parenting practices spans the region's urban middle class. The Singapore experience is but one instantiation of the wider sociotechnological landscape that is emerging from the intensifying use of mobile communication in the daily management of family life. Can we then consider transcendent parenting to have reared its head beyond Asia too? I boldly venture that it has because families worldwide are increasingly unified by their experience of mobile media being irrevocably woven into their everyday lives, just as families are bound by the fears and foibles that parents must confront as they raise their children in a fast-paced and rapidly changing world. Mine is by no means an audacious claim, because there is increasing evidence to show that transcendent parenting is emerging in many ways in virtually every corner of the globe. This is due to significant turns in the provision of education from elementary school through university in the face of heightened connectivity.

From the perspective of both schools and parents, the shared need for efficient and effective parent-school communication is becoming a key, nonnegotiable priority. In the United States, a survey by educational solutions provider Blackboard (2018) found that principals in the elementary and high schools are increasingly using social media tools to communicate with parents who in turn place a great premium on convenience, customization, and having information sent to them rather than being required to seek it. The report, illuminatingly subtitled "Text, Twitter, email, call—new expectations for school-to-home communications" drew attention to the need for schools to cater to "the needs of parents who are increasingly tech-savvy and value greater communications with their child's teacher and school." Indeed, as Julie Lythcott-Haims laments in *How to Raise an Adult*, the United States has become afflicted with an "achievement culture" (2015, 3) that motivates parents to pay greater attention to their children's academic performance, often to an unhealthy degree. She relates how a divorced couple who share joint custody of their son are mired in constant tension over the extent of parental involvement in his schoolwork: "Don's ex-wife calls to tell him to go on to the parent portal and check what's due in their son's classes, to make sure he turned in all his work, and to call the teacher if there's a discrepancy between what their son says he's done and what the online system indicates. Don sighs heavily as he relays this" (2015, 122). Such accounts reflect the growing shift in parent-school communication toward the use of such comprehensive, data-rich digital infrastructures, and the systemic and systematic enlistment of parents into the children's academic tasks that necessarily encourages transcendent parenting.

In Europe, also with its own particular mobile media usage patterns, transcendent parenting has also emerged from the growing use of home-school conferencing apps. In a column in Tes News, the online news portal of the Times Educational Supplement, a British primary school teacher lamented that British parents were increasingly using closed messaging features in apps such as Bambizo, ClassDoJo, and Edmodo to contact teachers throughout the day. These run the gamut from more trivial requests such as asking teachers to convey messages to their children, to weightier demands such as holding teachers to account for why their children lost participation points on ClassDojo. The author acknowledged that while these apps do provide a viable channel for parents and teachers to share useful information, the abuses she described "serve only to fuel a form of precision-parenting that slowly chips away at a child's long-term resilience" (Budden 2018). Another column by a parent in the same news portal detailed the sheer volume of information she was deluged with relating to her three children and their three schools (Henderson 2018). These included notifications via the school newsletters, school apps, three different WhatsApp groups, ClassDojo accounts, school websites, Tapestry (an app for tracking the child's development), on top of hardcopy letters.

Essentially therefore, notable commonalities course through the educational experiences of urban middle-class families around the world. The mobile media-rich landscape envelopes parents and children, powering and lubricating their household coordination. Beyond the home, the family is in turn communicating with schools, day care, and enrichment centers as well as other households, again leveraging the constant connectivity of mobile media that enables the liberal transmission of audio, video, visual, and textual information. This hyper-connected, media-rich, data-dense climate thus allows transcendent parenting to emerge, intensified by the societal valorization of children's academic achievements and the rising expectations around parenting.

NEGOTIATING THE CONSEQUENCES OF TRANSCENDENT PARENTING

Given these characteristics of our current sociotechnological landscape, must families yield to transcendent parenting practices? This also raises the question—don't parents themselves desire and appreciate transcendent parenting? Don't they wish to be available to all of their children, all of the time? As the evidence I shared throughout the book shows, parents are ultimately conflicted about this. While they may be gratified by their ability to offer support at the chime of a phone notification, they also feel pressured and at times overwhelmed by this need to always be on call.

Clearly, families differ in the extent to which parents engage in transcendent parenting, and yet they do not live in a vacuum and they do, mutually influence one another. With cultural constructions of parenting changing, due in part to the growing use of mobile communication in the execution of parenting duties, the norms around "ideal parenting" are also shifting. Just as mothers who interact online via discussion forums and blogs can shape norms about what it means to be a good parent (see for example Geinger, Vandenbroeck, and Roets 2014; Friedman 2010), mobile-enabled, child-parent, parent-parent, and parent-teacher communication also influence and reify norms about desirable parenting. As some parents explained earlier in the book, they did not feel that they could afford to ignore these parent chats or gradebook notifications for fear that their children would be disadvantaged. Similarly, the information being shared on what other parents were doing to support their children's academic pursuits translated into a sense of peer pressure for some. Such openly shared information effectively accrues toward social norms that are tantamount to a form of cultural hegemony, pressuring parents to engage in transcendent parenting, even if they are reluctant to bear the additional burden. Little wonder then that the weight of societal expectations surrounding parenting, as well as the impossibility of meeting them, leads people to feel ambivalent about parenthood (Brown 2010; Furedi 2008).

Besides feeling the pressure to conform, transcendent parenting does involve a concrete investment of time and energy that may progressively take its toll. Research on causes of exhaustion among overworked employees identifies factors such as rigidity coupled with unpredictability, fast pace, and tight deadlines, as well as availability 24/7 (Hewlett 2007). These factors could just as well be used to describe parenting given the rigorous standards around homework and examinations, the hectic school schedules, and parents feeling the need to always be there for their children. With transcendent parenting entering the picture, will parents find the strain of their obligations more onerous? Furthermore, the practical burden may yet be eclipsed by the emotional burden. As Lynn Clark astutely observed, parenting in the digital age involves a considerable degree of emotion work where parents need to sensitively strike a balance between involvement and interference (Clark 2013). At the same time, excessively active interference by parents in their children's peer interactions and disputes further circumscribes children's abilities to develop a healthy "potential space" from their parents and may impede their maturation (Winnicott 1990; 2005). Parents thus have the additional moral responsibility to carefully calibrate their interventions to avoid infringing on their children's privacy and grant them the agency to engage in independent problem-solving, so as to hone their ability to interpret and respond to social situations (boyd 2008).

Beyond the social realm, does the parental instinct to protect the child lead to a greater propensity for parents to step in when their child faces the slightest modicum of risk, to swoop in and whisk the child to safety when straying ever so slightly into harm's way? Furedi (2008) argues that children who are accustomed to "parenting on demand" have no opportunities to reflect on their own experiences and can become excessively self-centered. On their part, parents who provide parenting on demand will find themselves exhausted in keeping up this child-centered life rather than striking a necessary balance with adult-oriented activities. When children encounter risks, they are challenged in ways that enhance their personal development. Through risks and experimentation, children are given the opportunity to grow (Vygotsky 1978). If children are overprotected, they miss out on encounters where they can develop "the risk-taker's advantage" (Ungar 2007). He argues that in order to mature well, children need adventure and responsibility, both of which are accompanied by risk. Hence, rather than protect children from all real and perceived dangers, parents need to strike a fine balance between exercising vigilance in the face of genuine risks and giving children the space to experience some risky activities that can empower them. When children experience and manage risks on their own, they exercise personal competencies and experience self-efficacy. When working with others to tackle risks, they can demonstrate empathy, practice social interaction, and feel a sense of community with and responsibility for others. Risk is therefore an essential ingredient in a young person's healthy maturation. By this token, children who are perpetually connected to their parents, all the way from childhood into adulthood, do not have sufficient opportunities to experience risks and to mature from the experience of managing risks.

After all, in as much as these technologies pave the way for parents to keep an eye on their children through every stage of their maturation, what remains to be seen are the long-term effects such overprotection can have on children and their development into independent, autonomous adults. These technologies can facilitate (and exacerbate) overprotection and, indeed, lengthen the period for which parents must provide oversight and guidance. Young people then remain "parented" even as they enter their adult years. This is compounded by shifts in the developmental trajectory of young people around the world. With the prolonging of childhood and the delay in the onset of adulthood, parental oversight during emerging adulthood prevails in many urban middle-class households. In particular, with the growing importance of higher education, young people are increasing the amount of time they spend in formal education, followed by a period of experimenting with different roles after graduation, before eventually deciding on a desired career that is both well-paying and personally fulfilling. This is quite unlike their parents who had settled in long-term jobs at an early age and who viewed marriage and parenthood as "achievements to be pursued" (Arnett 2004, 6). Consequently, whereas their parents had made serious lifelong decisions associated with adulthood at a comparatively early age, the path toward adulthood is a much longer one for young people today.

THROUGH THE SMARTPHONE GLASS

In this book, I have principally focused on how mobile communication has engendered the conditions for transcendent parenting practices to emerge, thereby transforming family life. I have alluded at points to how transcendent parenting practices, themselves rooted in parenting priorities, have in turn shaped the trajectory of mobile communication services that directly support parenting. I wish to therefore conclude here by contemplating the mutually constitutive, spiraling relationship (MacKenzie and Wajcman 1999) between mobile communication and parenting.

The parenting priorities of Asian parents, shaped by long-held cultural valorizations of parental nurturing, parental oversight, and academic excellence in children, impel the use of mobile communication in particular ways that both address and reinforce these priorities. But the transcendent parenting practices that emerge from this sociocultural climate are simultaneously casting the uses of mobile communication in the molds of omnipresence, surveillance, dependency, oversharing, and relentlessness, and a seeming acceptance of them all. As Judy Wajcman observed, "technologies bear the imprint of the people and social context in which they develop" (2015, 29).

Indeed, we have seen how the technologies of transcendent parenting construct family life, primarily by altering perceptions of space and time. As Leopoldina Fortunati argues, "the mobile is changing not only society, but above all the framework in which society lives. This framework is made up of space and time as its primary determinations" (2002, 513). Mobile communication helps parents transcend the work and domestic spaces to be ever present in their children's lives, even if not in direct physical propinquity. This then necessitates that they parent relentlessly, as they remain in perpetual contact with their children and other significant parties. Rich Ling observed, "the mobile phone has become taken for granted. It has become woven into our expectations of one another" (2012, xi), and the mutual expectations between parents and children have been thus determined for the mobile age. In domesticating and deploying mobile communication in the minutiae of their daily coordination and interactions, parents and children thus reshape their family culture. Children are socialized into their roles and obligations within the family, and definitions of what parents must do for their children are both reflected in and legitimated by their mobile communication practices. Rather than just serving as a communication tool therefore, the mobile phone is a veritable "meaning making device" (Caronia 2008, 117), allowing parents and children to both understand and build the very foundations of their familial ties.

In turn, these meanings that families have inscribed into their mobile communication practices also shape technological infrastructures. More specialized platforms, apps, and services are being introduced for parents to manage family schedules, fulfill their children's educational obligations, support their children's learning, guide their children's media use, exercise surveillance and oversight, and protect their children from risk and harm. As these innovations gain traction, their intensifying use will constitute a growing component of parenting obligations, thereby altering our conceptions of what it means to be a good parent.

When we look through the smartphone glass and into the future therefore, ruminating over the ways in which families engage with and through mobile technologies, we need to ponder how well we are coping with these sociotechnological transformations. We should also reflect on the cultural significance of what appear at first brush to be merely technological encounters between users and interfaces. Each mobile-facilitated exchange that links parents to children, parents to parents, and schools to homes serves to gradually redefine what it means to be a parent and which parenting practices we valorize. Indeed, as we come to terms with the ineluctable presence of mobile communication in family life, we must also recognize this discernible shift toward transcendent parenting, remind parents to tame the swelling impulse toward over-involvement, and grant children the space they need to grow.

APPENDIX

METHODS

I present here a description of the research method used for the two key studies that constitute the main findings on which this book is based. My fieldwork and data analysis depart from the technology domestication perspective that I have always found provides a flexible yet encompassing framework by which to appreciate the influence of technology on family life. The first study, conducted between July and November 2016, was on the use of tablets and touchscreen devices in families with preschoolers. I utilized semi-structured, face-to-face interviews, and observations after obtaining institutional ethical approval, and I conducted the research with the help of trained research assistants. These interviews were all conducted in the homes of the respondents whom we recruited through snowballing from the initial wave of respondents we recruited, as well as via posts shared through social media such as Facebook. We would typically begin by interviewing the preschooler's mother for about 50 to 75 minutes, before observing the preschooler's interactions with the tablet device in the mother's presence for 10 to 15 minutes. This allowed us to observe the home environment and the natural setting in which these preschoolers use digital devices. As mothers bear more responsibility for childrearing in the typical patriarchal Asian family, mothers were chosen as interviewees over fathers. Nevertheless, we would capture the father's input if he happened to be present during the interview and voluntarily offered his views.

The interview questions sought to understand reasons for acquiring different mobile devices for the home, the mother's views on the media, the child's daily activities, and patterns of using mobile devices and other forms of media at home and at school. We also inquired about the influence of other people or social factors on the child's device use and any other topic that became salient as the interview progressed. Meanwhile, we also took observational notes of the home environment, the availability of media devices, the child's interaction with devices, and mother-child interactions. Interviews were captured with an audio recorder and ended with an "apps-ploration" exercise in which the mother was asked to show the researcher the tablet's contents, specifically the different apps used by the child and the mother's motivations for installing them. We also made observations of the home's physical environment, with special attention paid to locations in the home where the tablet was stored and used by the child, the child's play areas, and his/her favorite toys. Photographs of the phone apps and the home were also taken.

In the second part of the research, we observed the child's interactions with the tablet device and/or mobile phones in the mother's presence and took notes of the child's actions on the devices, the child's spoken words, the apps they used, and the duration of time they spent on the device. Photographs of the mother and child during the observation session were taken from an angle to prevent identification. Upon completing the research, each mother-child dyad was reimbursed with a grocery voucher that could cover the cost of approximately half a week's groceries for an average Singapore family, or SGD$50. The respondents were recruited through purposive- and snowball-sampling methods via personal networks and had to be Singapore citizens/residents who owned and used touchscreen tablet devices. The mother had to be aged 21 and above, and the child had to be between 3- and 5-years-old at the time of the research. Our final sample included 40 mother-child dyads in Singapore, but the mothers were also welcome to share experiences related to their other children who were not necessarily preschoolers. The interviews were fully transcribed into English.

The second fieldwork component was interviews with 30 Singaporean parents between February and March 2018 to understand their use of mobile phone apps in parenting their school-going children. We interviewed parents and took photographs of their mobile devices, their phone contents, and specifically the relevant apps. The interviews were mostly conducted in the respondents' homes but, occasionally, at the respondents' request, were held in public venues such as cafés. The interviews also probed into respondents' general attitudes toward parenting, education, and technology. Due to the intrusive nature of the research, respondents were reimbursed with a grocery voucher that could cover the cost of approximately half a week's groceries for an average Singapore family, or SGD$50. Respondents were recruited through purposive- and snowball-sampling methods via announcements shared over personal and social media networks that sought the participation of families in Singapore with school-going children with prior experience of owning touchscreen tablet devices. We also captured the interviewees' spouses' input if they happened to be present during the interview and voluntarily offered their views.

In total, 70 parents with 163 children were interviewed for the two combined fieldwork components.

BIBLIOGRAPHY

Chapter 1

Castells, Manuel. 1996. *The Rise of the Network Society, The Information Age: Economy, Society and Culture*. Vol. 1. Oxford: Blackwell.

Choi, Kimburley WY. 2016. "On the fast track to a head start: A visual ethnographic study of parental consumption of children's play and learning activities in Hong Kong." *Childhood* 23 (1): 123–139. doi:10.1177/0907568215586838

Ebbeck, Marjory, Hoi Yin Bonnie Yim, Yvonne Chan, and Mandy Goh. 2016. "Singaporean parents' views of their young children's access and use of technological devices." *Early Childhood Education Journal* 44 (2): 127–134. doi:10.1007/s10643-015-0695-4

Euromonitor International. 2017. "Penetration rates for consumer electronics." Closed database.

Gentzler, Amy L., Ann M. Oberhauser, David Westerman, and Danielle K. Nadorff. 2011. "College students' use of electronic communication with parents: Links to loneliness, attachment, and relationship quality." *Cyberpsychology, Behavior, and Social Networking* 14 (1-2): 71–74. doi:10.1089/cyber.2009.0409

Harrison, Kristen. 2015. "Media and the family." *Journal of Children and Media* 9 (1): 1–4. doi:10.1080/17482798.2015.997513.

Hendriyani, Ed Hollander, Leen d'Haenens, and Johannes Beentjes. 2014. "Views on children's media use in Indonesia: Parents, children, and teachers." *International Communication Gazette* 76 (4-5): 322–339. doi:10.1177/1748048514523527

Hjorth, Larissa, Heather Horst, Sarah Pink, Baohua Zhou, Fumitoshi Kato, Genevieve Bell, Kana Ohashi, Chris Malmo, and Miao Xiao. 2016. "Locating the mobile: Intergenerational locative media in Tokyo, Shanghai and Melbourne."

In *Lifestyle Media in Asia: Consumption, Aspiration and Identity*, edited by Fran Martin and Tania Lewis, 147–161. London: Routledge.

Hochschild, Arlie, and Anne Machung. 2012. *The Second Shift: Working Families and the Revolution at Home*. New York: Penguin.

Hong, Helen, Elizabeth Koh, Jason Loh, Chun Ming Tan, and Hui Mien Tan. 2016. "Exploring parental involvement in smartphone-enabled learning." In *Future Learning in Primary Schools: A Singapore Perspective*, edited by Ching Sing Chai, Cher Ping Lim, and Chun Ming Tan, 159–176. Singapore: Springer Science+Business Media.

Jennings, Nancy. 2017. "Media and families: Looking ahead." *Journal of Family Communication* 17 (3): 203–207. doi: 10.1080/15267431.2017.1322972

Jiow, Hee Jhee, and Sun Sun Lim. 2012. "The evolution of video game affordances and implications for parental mediation." *Bulletin of Science, Technology & Society* 32 (6): 455–462. doi:10.1177/0270467612469077

Kwon, Min, Dai-Jin Kim, Hyun Cho, and Soo Yang. 2013. "The smartphone addiction scale: Development and validation of a short version for adolescents." *PloS One* 8 (12): e83558. doi:10.1371/journal.pone.0083558

Lim, Sun Sun, and Becky Pham. 2016. "'If you are a foreigner in a foreign country, you stick together': Technologically mediated communication and acculturation of migrant students." *New Media & Society* 18 (10): 2171–2188. doi:10.1177/1461444816655612

Ling, Rich, and Troels Fibæk Bertel. 2013. "Mobile communication culture among children and adolescents." In *Routledge International Handbook of Children, Adolescents and Media*, edited by Dafna Lemish, 127–133. New York: Routledge.

McDonald, Tom. 2016. "Desiring mobiles, desiring education: Mobile phones and families in a rural Chinese Town." In *Mobile Communication and the Family—Asian Experiences in Technology Domestication*, edited by Sun Sun Lim, 13–32. Dordrecht: Springer.

Pham, Becky, and Sun Sun Lim. 2016. "Empowering interactions, sustaining ties: Vietnamese migrant students' communication with left-behind family and friends." In *Mobile Communication and the Family—Asian Experiences in Technology Domestication*, edited by Sun Sun Lim, 109–126. Dordrecht: Springer.

Rahayu, and Sun Sun Lim. 2016. "Balancing religion, technology and parenthood: Indonesian Muslim mothers' supervision of children's Internet use." In *Mobile Communication and the Family—Asian Experiences in Technology Domestication*, edited by Sun Sun Lim, 33–50. Dordrecht: Springer.

Sekarasih, Laras. 2016. "Restricting, distracting, and reasoning: Parental mediation of young children's use of mobile communication technology in Indonesia." In *Mobile Communication and the Family—Asian Experiences in Technology Domestication*, edited by Sun Sun Lim, 129–146. Dordrecht: Springer.

Seo, Hogeun, and Claire Shinhea Lee. 2017. "Emotion matters: What happens between young children and parents in a touch screen world." *International Journal of Communication* 11 (2017): 561–580.

Simonds, Dave. 2018. "What other countries can learn from Singapore's schools." *The Economist*, August 12. Accessed March 10, 2019. https://www.economist.com/leaders/2018/08/30/what-other-countries-can-learn-from-singapores-schools

Tan, Ern Ser. 2015. "Class and social orientations: Key findings from the Social Stratification Survey 2011." Singapore: Institute of Policy Studies.

Tan, Ern Ser, and Min Wei Tan. 2016. "Two stories on class in Singapore: Diversity or division?" In *Managing Diversity in Singapore*, edited by Mathew Mathews and Wai Fong Chiang, 121–141. Singapore: Institute of Policy Studies and World Scientific.

We Are Social. 2017. "Digital in 2017: Global overview." Accessed May 30, 2018. https://wearesocial.com/special-reports/digital-in-2017-global-overview

Winstedt, Richard Olof, Robert Ho, Annajane Kennard, and Thomas R. Leinbach. 2019. "Singapore." *Encyclopaedia Britannica*. Accessed March 10, 2019. https://www.britannica.com/place/Singapore

Wu, Cynthia Sau Ting, Cathrine Fowler, Winsome Yuk Yin Lam, Ho Ting Wong, Charmaine Hei Man Wong, and Alice Yuen Loke. 2014. "Parenting approaches and digital technology use of preschool age children in a Chinese community." *Italian Journal of Pediatrics* 40 (44). doi:10.1186/1824-7288-40-44

Chapter 2

Barr, Michael D., and Zlatko Skrbiš. 2008. *Constructing Singapore: Elitism, Ethnicity and the Nation-Building Project*. Copenhagen, Denmark: NIAS Press.

Bray, Mark, and Chad Lykins. 2012. *Shadow Education: Private Supplementary Tutoring and Its Implications for Policy Makers in Asia*. The Philippines: Asian Development Bank.

Bristow, Jennie. 2014. "The double bind of parenting culture: Helicopter parents and cotton wool kids." In *Parenting Culture Studies*, edited by Ellie Lee, Jennie Bristow, Charlotte Faircloth, and Jan Macvarish, 200–222. UK: Palgrave Macmillan.

Chao, Ruth, and Vivian Tseng. 2005. "Parenting of Asians." In *Handbook of Parenting: Volume 4: Social Conditions and Applied Parenting*, edited by Marc H. Bornstein, 59–94. New Jersey: Lawrence Erlbaum Associates.

Chao, Ruth K. 1995. "Chinese and European American cultural models of the self reflected in mothers' childrearing beliefs." *Ethos* 23: 328–354. doi:10.1525/eth.1995.23.3.02a00030

Chen, Fu-Mei, and Tom Luster. 2002. "Factors related to parenting practices in Taiwan." *Early Child Development and Care* 172 (5): 413–430. doi:10.1080/03004430214549

Choi, Kimburley WY. 2016. "On the fast track to a head start: A visual ethnographic study of parental consumption of children's play and learning activities in Hong Kong." *Childhood* 23 (1): 123–139. doi:10.1177/0907568215586838

Chua, Amy. 2011. *Battle Hymn of the Tiger Mother*. London: Bloomsbury.

Clark, Lynn Schofield. 2013. *The Parent App: Understanding Families in the Digital Age*. New York: Oxford University Press.

Clarke, Christine. 2001. "The role of parents in Singapore primary schools." *Teaching and Learning* 22 (2): 83–92.

Domina, Thurston. 2005. "Leveling the home advantage: Assessing the effectiveness of parental involvement in elementary school." *Sociology of Education* 78 (3): 233–249.

Epstein, Joyce L. 1995. "School/family/community partnerships." *Phi Delta Kappan* 76 (9): 701–712.

Faircloth, Charlotte. 2014. "Intensive parenting and the expansion of parenting." In *Parenting Culture Studies*, edited by Ellie Lee, Jennie Bristow, Charlotte Faircloth, and Jan Macvarish, 25–50. UK: Palgrave Macmillan.

Fan, Xitao, and Michael Chen. 2001. "Parental involvement and students' academic achievement: A meta-analysis." *Educational Psychology Review* 13 (1): 1–22. doi:10.1023/A:1009048817385

Frank, Robert H. 1985. "The demand for unobservable and other nonpositional goods." *The American Economic Review* 75 (1): 101–116.

Furedi, Frank. 2002. *Culture of Fear: Risk-taking and the Morality of Low Expectation*. Revised edition. London: Continuum.

Furedi, Frank. 2008. *Paranoid Parenting: Why Ignoring the Experts May Be Best for Your Child*. London: Continuum.

Gee, Christopher. 2012. "The educational 'arms race': All for one, loss for all." IPS Working Papers No. 20. Singapore: Institute of Policy Studies (IPS). Accessed May 30, 2018. http://lkyspp2.nus.edu.sg/ips/wp-content/uploads/sites/2/2013/06/wp20.pdf

Godwin, Richard. 2019. "'You can track everything': The parents who digitise their babies' lives." *The Guardian*, March 2. Accessed March 2, 2019. https://www.theguardian.com/lifeandstyle/2019/mar/02/apps-that-track-babies-and-give-data-to-tech-firms-parents

Gonzalez-DeHass, Alyssa R., Patricia P. Willems, and Marie F. Doan Holbein. 2005. "Examining the relationship between parental involvement and student motivation." *Educational Psychology Review* 17 (2): 99–123. doi:10.1007/s10648-005-3949-7

Göransson, Kristina. 2015. "Raising successful children: Children as accumulation strategy and the renegotiation of parenting arrangements in Singapore." *The Asia Pacific Journal of Anthropology* 16 (3): 211–226. doi:10.1080/14442213.2015.1028431

Gorman, Jean Cheng. 1998. "Parenting attitudes and practices of immigrant Chinese mothers of adolescents." *Family Relations* 47 (1): 73–80.

Hau, Kit-Tai, and Farideh Salili. 1991. "Structure and semantic differential placement of specific causes: Academic causal attributions by Chinese students in Hong Kong." *International Journal of Psychology* 26 (2): 175–193.

Hays, Sharon. 1996. *The Cultural Contradictions of Motherhood*. New Haven: Yale University Press.

Heiman, Rachel, Mark Liechty, and Carla Freeman. 2012. "Introduction: Charting an anthropology of the middle-classes." In *The Global Middle Classes: Theorizing through Ethnography*, edited by Rachel Heiman, Carla Freeman, and Mark Liechty, 3–29. Santa Fe: SAR Press.

Hill, Nancy E., and Lorraine C. Taylor. 2004. "Parental school involvement and children's academic achievement: Pragmatics and issues." *Current Directions in Psychological Science* 13 (4): 161–164. doi:10.1111/j.0963-7214.2004.00298.x

Ho, David Y., and Tsi Kit Kang. 1984. "Intergenerational comparisons of child-rearing attitudes and practices in Hong Kong." *Developmental Psychology* 20 (6): 1004–1016.

Hunt, Alan. 2003. "Risk and moralization in everyday life." In *Risk and Morality*, edited by Richard Victor Ericson and Aaron Doyle, 165–192. Toronto: University of Toronto Press.

Karsten, Lia. 2015. "Middle-class childhood and parenting culture in high-rise Hong Kong: On scheduled lives, the school trap and a new urban idyll." *Children's Geographies* 13 (5): 556–570. doi:10.1080/14733285.2014.915288

Katz, Cindi. 2008. "Childhood as spectacle: Relays of anxiety and the reconfiguration of the child." *Cultural Geographies* 15 (1): 5–17. doi:10.1177/1474474007085773

Katz, Timothy Z., Patricia B. Keith, Gretchen C. Troutman, and Patricia G. Bickley. 1993. "Does parental involvement affect eighth-grade student achievement? Structural analysis of national data." *School Psychology Review* 22 (3): 474–496.

Katz, Vikki S., and Carmen Gonzalez. 2016. "Community variations in low-income Latino families' technology adoption and integration." *American Behavioral Scientist* 60 (1): 59–80. doi:10.1177/0002764215601712

Kelley, Michelle L., and Hui-Mei Tseng. 1992. "Cultural differences in child rearing: A comparison of immigrant Chinese and Caucasian American mothers." *Journal of Cross-Cultural Psychology* 23 (4): 444–455.

Kibria, Nazli. 1993. *Family Tightrope: The Changing Lives of Vietnamese Americans*. Princeton, NJ: Princeton University Press.

Lareau, Annette. 2003. *Unequal Childhoods: Race, Class and Family Life*. Berkeley: University of California Press.

Leaver, Tama. 2017. "Intimate surveillance: Normalizing parental monitoring and mediation of infants online." *Social Media+ Society* 3 (2): 1–10. doi:10.1177/2056305117707192

Lee, Ellie. 2014. "Introduction." In *Parenting Culture Studies*, edited by Ellie Lee, Jennie Bristow, Charlotte Faircloth, and Jan Macvarish, 1–24. UK: Palgrave Macmillan.

Lee, Jungyoon, Heekeun Yu, and Sumi Choi. 2012. "The influences of parental acceptance and parental control on school adjustment and academic achievement for South Korean children: The mediation role of self-regulation." *Asia Pacific Education Review* 13 (2): 227–237. doi:10.1007/s12564-011-9186-5

Lim, Sun Sun, and Carol Soon. 2010. "The influence of social and cultural factors on mothers' domestication of household ICTs—Experiences of Chinese and Korean women." *Telematics and Informatics* 27 (3): 205–216. doi:10.1016/j.tele.2009.07.001

Lin, Huey-Ya. 1999. "Mothers' beliefs, goals and child-rearing behaviors (II): Questionnaire construction and correlation analysis." *Research in Applied Psychology* 3: 219–244.

Ling, Rich, and Birgitte Yttri. 2002. "Hyper-coordination via mobile phones in Norway." In *Perpetual Contact: Mobile Communication, Private Talk, Public Performance*, edited by James E. Katz and Mark Aakhus, 139–169. Cambridge: Cambridge University Press.

Livingstone, Sonia, and Alicia Blum-Ross. 2018. "Imagining the future through the lens of the digital: Parents' narratives of generational change." In *A Networked Self: Birth, Life, Death*, edited by Zizi Papacharissi, 50–68. New York: Routledge.

Lowinger, Robert Jay, and Heide Kwok. 2001. "Parental overprotection in Asian American children: A psychodynamic clinical perspective." *Psychotherapy: Theory, Research, Practice, Training* 38 (3): 319–330.

Luo, Wenshu, Khin Maung Aye, David Hogan, Berinderjeet Kaur, and Melvin Chee Yeen Chan. 2013. "Parenting behaviors and learning of Singapore students: The mediational role of achievement goals." *Motivation and Emotion* 37 (2): 274–285. doi:10.1007/s11031-012-9303-8

Lupton, Deborah, Sarah Pedersen, and Gareth M. Thomas. 2016. "Parenting and digital media: From the early web to contemporary digital society." *Sociology Compass* 10 (8): 730–743. doi:10.1111/soc4.12398

Matsuda, Misa. 2008. "Children with Keitai: When mobile phones change from 'unnecessary' to 'necessary.'" *East Asian Science, Technology and Society: An International Journal* 2 (2): 167–188. doi:10.1215/s12280-008-9050-9

McAdams, Dan P. 1993. *The stories We Live By: Personal Myths and the Making of the Self*. New York: Guilford.

Nelson, Margaret K. 2010. *Parenting out of Control: Anxious Parents in Uncertain Times*. New York: New York University Press.

Pham, Becky, and Sun Sun Lim. 2018. "Bridging parental expectations and children's aspirations: Creative strategies in migrant students' mediated communication with their left-behind families." In *Transnational Migrations in the Asia-Pacific*, edited by Catherine Gomes and Brenda S. A. Yeoh, 25–44. London: Rowman and Littlefield.

Pomerantz, Eva M., and Qian Wang. 2009. "The role of parental control in children's development in Western and East Asian countries." *Current Directions in Psychological Science* 18 (5): 285–289. doi:10.1111/j.1467-8721.2009.01653.x

Rakow, Lana F., and Vija Navarro. 1993. "Remote mothering and the parallel shift: Women meet the cellular telephone." *Critical Studies in Media Communication* 10 (2): 144–157. doi:10.1080/15295039309366856

Ribak, Rivka. 2009. "Remote control, umbilical cord and beyond: The mobile phone as a transitional object." *British Journal of Developmental Psychology* 27 (1): 183–196. doi:10.1348/026151008X388413

Salili, Farideh. 1996. "Accepting personal responsibility for learning." In *The Chinese Learner: Cultural, Psychological, and Contextual Influences*, edited by David A. Watkins and John Burville Biggs, 85–105. Hong Kong: Comparative Education Research Centre.

Salili, Farideh, Chi Yue Chiu, and Simon Lai. 2001. "The influence of culture and context on students' motivational orientation and performance." In *Student Motivation: The Culture and Context of Learning*, edited by Farideh Salili, Chi Yue Chiu, and Ying Yi Hong, 221–247. New York: Kluwer Academic/Plenum.

Shaw, Susan M. 2008. "Family leisure and changing ideologies of parenthood." *Sociology Compass* 2 (2): 688–703. doi:10.1111/j.1751-9020.2007.00076.x

Stright, Anne Dopkins, and Kim Lian Yeo. 2014. "Maternal parenting styles, school involvement, and children's school achievement and conduct in Singapore." *Journal of Educational Psychology* 106 (1): 301–314. doi:10.1037/a0033821

Tan, Charlene. 2017. "Private supplementary tutoring and parentocracy in Singapore." *Interchange* 48 (4): 315–329. doi:10.1007/s10780-017-9303-4

Tobin, Joseph Jay, David YH Wu, and Dana H. Davidson. 1991. *Preschool In Three Cultures: Japan, China, and the United States*. New Haven: Yale University Press.

Ungar, Michael. 2007. *Too Safe for Their Own Good: How Risk and Responsibility Help Teens Thrive*. Toronto: McClelland and Stewart.

Ungar, Michael. 2009. "Overprotective parenting: Helping parents provide children the right amount of risk and responsibility." *The American Journal of Family Therapy* 37 (3): 258–271. doi:10.1080/01926180802534247

Valkenburg, Patti M., and Jessica Taylor Piotrowski. 2017. *Plugged In: How Media Attract and Affect Youth*. New Haven: Yale University Press.

Waterson, Roxana, and Deepak Kumar Behera. 2011. "Introduction: Extending ethnographic research with children in the Asia-Pacific region." *The Asia Pacific Journal of Anthropology* 12 (5): 411–425. doi:10.1080/14442213.2011.611163

Weisskirch, Robert S. 2009. "Parenting by cell phone: Parental monitoring of adolescents and family relations." *Journal of Youth and Adolescence* 38 (8): 1123–1139. doi:10.1007/s10964-008-9374-8

Wilson, Julie A., and Emily Chivers Yochim. 2017. *Mothering through Precarity: Women's Work and Digital Media*. Durham: Duke University Press.

Winstedt, Richard Olof, Robert Ho, Annajane Kennard, and Thomas R. Leinbach. 2019. "Singapore." *Encyclopaedia Britannica*. Accessed March 10, 2019. https://www.britannica.com/place/Singapore

Wise, Amanda. 2016. "Behind the world's best students is a soul-crushing, billion-dollar private education industry." *Yahoo! News*, December 12. Accessed May 30, 2018. https://sg.news.yahoo.com/behind-world-best-students-soul-022157417.html

Wolf, Joan B. 2010. *Is Breast Best? Taking on the Breastfeeding Experts and the New High Stakes of Motherhood.* New York: New York University Press.

Xiong, Zha Blong, Patricia A. Eliason, Daniel F. Detzner, and Michael J. Cleveland. 2005. "Southeast Asian immigrants' perceptions of good adolescents and good parents." *The Journal of Psychology* 139 (2): 159–175. doi:10.3200/JRLP.139.2.159-175

Xu, Zhengyuan, Wan Chuan Wen, Paul Mussen, Shen Jian-Xian, Li Chang-Min, and Cao Zi-Fang. 1991. "Family socialization and children's behavior and personality development in China." *The Journal of Genetic Psychology* 152 (2): 239–253.

Yeoh, Brenda S. A., and Shirlena Huang. 2010. "Mothers on the move: Children's education and transnational mobility in global-city Singapore." In *The Globalization of Motherhood: Deconstructions and Reconstructions of Biology and Care*, edited by Wendy Chavkin and JaneMaree Maher, 31–54. London: Routledge.

Zelizer, Viviana A. 1994. *Pricing the Priceless Child: The Changing Social Value of Children.* Princeton, NJ: Princeton University Press.

Chapter 3

Barr, Michael D., and Zlatko Skrbiš. 2008. *Constructing Singapore: Elitism, Ethnicity and the Nation-building Project.* Copenhagen, Denmark: NIAS Press.

Bray, Mark, and Chad Lykins. 2012. *Shadow Education: Private Supplementary Tutoring and Its Implications for Policy Makers in Asia.* The Philippines: Asian Development Bank.

Chaboudy, Russell, and Paula Jameson. 2001. "Connecting families and schools through technology." *Book Report* 20 (2): 52–57.

Chen, Fu-Mei, and Tom Luster. 2002. "Factors related to parenting practices in Taiwan." *Early Child Development and Care* 172 (5): 413–430. doi:10.1080/03004430214549

Clark, Sheryl, Anna Mountford-Zimdars, and Becky Francis. 2015. "Risk, choice and social disadvantage: Young people's decision-making in a marketised higher education system." *Sociological Research Online* 20 (3): 1–14. doi:10.5153/sro.3727

Clarke, Christine. 2001. "The role of parents in Singapore primary schools." *Teaching and Learning* 22 (2): 83–92.

Chao, Ruth, and Vivian Tseng. 2005. "Parenting of Asians." In *Handbook of Parenting: Volume 4: Social Conditions and Applied Parenting*, edited by Marc H. Bornstein, 59–94. New Jersey: Lawrence Erlbaum Associates.

Chao, Ruth K. 1995. "Chinese and European American Cultural models of the self reflected in mothers' childrearing beliefs." *Ethos* 23: 328–354. doi:10.1525/eth.1995.23.3.02a00030

Faircloth, Charlotte. 2014. "Intensive parenting and the expansion of parenting." In *Parenting Culture Studies*, edited by Ellie Lee, Jennie Bristow, Charlotte Faircloth, and Jan Macvarish, 25–50. UK: Palgrave Macmillan.

Fan, Xitao, and Michael Chen. 2001. "Parental involvement and students' academic achievement: A meta-analysis." *Educational Psychology Review* 13 (1): 1–22. doi:10.1023/A:1009048817385

Furedi, Frank. 2002. *Culture of Fear: Risk-taking and the Morality of Low Expectation*. Revised edition. London: Continuum.

Gee, Christopher. 2012. "The educational 'arms race': All for one, loss for all." IPS Working Papers No. 20. Singapore: Institute of Policy Studies (IPS). Accessed 30 May, 2018. http://lkyspp2.nus.edu.sg/ips/wp-content/uploads/sites/2/2013/06/wp20.pdf

Göransson, Kristina. 2015. "Raising successful children: Children as accumulation strategy and the renegotiation of parenting arrangements in Singapore." *The Asia Pacific Journal of Anthropology* 16 (3): 211–226. doi:10.1080/14442213.2015.1028431

Hau, Kit-Tai, and Farideh Salili. 1991. "Structure and semantic differential placement of specific causes: Academic causal attributions by Chinese students in Hong Kong." *International Journal of Psychology* 26 (2): 175–193.

Hays, Sharon. 1996. *The Cultural Contradictions of Motherhood*. New Haven: Yale University Press.

Henderson, Anne T., and Karen L. Mapp. 2002. *A New Wave of Evidence: The Impact of School, Family, and Community Connections on Student Achievement—Annual Synthesis, 2002*. Texas: National Center for Family & Community Connections with Schools.

Katz, Cindi. 2008. "Childhood as spectacle: Relays of anxiety and the reconfiguration of the child." *Cultural Geographies* 15 (1): 5–17. doi:10.1177/1474474007085773

Lareau, Annette. 2003. *Unequal Childhoods: Race, Class and Family Life*. Berkeley: University of California Press.

Nelson, Margaret K. 2010. *Parenting out of Control: Anxious Parents in Uncertain Times*. New York: New York University Press.

Rakow, Lana and Vija Navarro. 1993. "Remote mothering and the parallel shift: Women meet the cellular telephone." *Critical Studies in Mass Communication* 10 (2): 144–157.

Salili, Farideh. 1996. "Accepting personal responsibility for learning." In *The Chinese Learner: Cultural, Psychological, and Contextual Influences*, edited by David A. Watkins and John Burville Biggs, 85–105. Hong Kong: Comparative Education Research Centre.

Saw, Anne, Howard Berenbaum, and Sumie Okazaki. "Influences of personal standards and perceived parental expectations on worry for Asian American and white American college students." *Anxiety, Stress & Coping* 26 (2): 187–202. doi:10.1080/10615806.2012.668536

Teo, You Yenn. 2018. "Commentary: Why investing in early childhood education cannot be the primary solution to inequality." *Channel NewsAsia*, May 9. Accessed May 30, 2018. https://www.channelnewsasia.com/news/commentary/early-education-tackling-inequality-teo-you-yenn-10213584

Wolf, Joan B. 2010. *Is Breast Best? Taking on the Breastfeeding Experts and the New High Stakes of Motherhood*. New York: New York University Press.

Yeoh, Brenda S. A., and Shirlena Huang. 2010. "Mothers on the move: Children's education and transnational mobility in global-city Singapore." In *The Globalization of Motherhood: Deconstructions and Reconstructions of Biology and Care*, edited by Wendy Chavkin and JaneMaree Maher, 31–54. London: Routledge.

Chapter 4

Blackerby, John M., Jr. 2005. "Effective communication: Opening lines of communication with email." Master's thesis, Valdosta State University.

Faircloth, Charlotte. 2014. "Intensive parenting and the expansion of parenting." In *Parenting Culture Studies*, edited by Ellie Lee, Jennie Bristow, Charlotte Faircloth, and Jan Macvarish, 25–50. UK: Palgrave Macmillan.

Furedi, Frank. 2002. *Culture of Fear: Risk-taking and the Morality of Low Expectation*. Revised edition. London: Continuum.

Furedi, Frank. 2008. *Paranoid Parenting: Why Ignoring the Experts May Be Best for Your Child*. London: Continuum.

Hays, Sharon. 1996. *The Cultural Contradictions of Motherhood*. New Haven: Yale University Press.

Lareau, Annette. 2003. *Unequal Childhoods: Race, Class and Family Life*. Berkeley: University of California Press.

Morris, Vivian Gunn, Satomi Izumi-Taylor, Cheri Lewis Smith, and Denise L. Winsor. 2010. "Promoting family involvement through using technology." In *Technology for Early Childhood Education and Socialization: Developmental Applications and Methodologies*, edited by Sally Blake and Satomi Izumi-Taylor, 149–161. Hershey, PA: IGI Global.

Nelson, Margaret K. 2010. *Parenting out of Control: Anxious Parents in Uncertain Times*. New York: New York University Press.

Pakter, Alexander, and Li-Ling Chen. 2013. "The daily text: Increasing parental involvement in education with mobile text messaging." *Journal of Educational Technology Systems* 41 (4): 353–367. doi: 10.2190/ET.41.4.f

Stright, Anne Dopkins, and Kim Lian Yeo. 2014. "Maternal parenting styles, school involvement, and children's school achievement and conduct in Singapore." *Journal of Educational Psychology* 106 (1): 301–314. doi:10.1037/a0033821

Thompson, Blair Christopher, Joseph P. Mazer, and Elizabeth Flood Grady. 2015. "The changing nature of parent–teacher communication: Mode selection in the smartphone era." *Communication Education* 64 (2): 187–207. doi:10.1080/03634523.2015.1014382

Wabisabi Learning. 2014. "12 apps for smarter teacher-parent communication." Accessed March 10, 2019. https://www.wabisabilearning.com/blog/12-apps-for-smarter-teacher-parent-communication

Yeoh, Brenda S. A., and Shirlena Huang. 2010. "Mothers on the move: Children's education and transnational mobility in global-city Singapore." In *The Globalization of Motherhood: Deconstructions and Reconstructions of Biology and Care*, edited by Wendy Chavkin and JaneMaree Maher, 31–54. London: Routledge.

Zieger, Laura Bardroff, and Jennifer Tan. 2012. "Improving parental involvement in secondary schools through communication technology." *Journal of Literacy and Technology* 13 (1): 30–54.

Chapter 5

AppAnnie. n.d. Accessed October 30, 2017. https://www.appannie.com/en/apps/google-play/top/singapore/application/parenting/

Caronia, Letizia. 2008. "Growing up wireless: Being a parent and being a child in the age of mobile communication." In *Digital Literacy: Tools and Methodologies for Information Society*, edited by Pier Cesare Rivoltella, 99–125. Hershey, PA: IGI Global. doi:10.4018/978-1-59904-798-0.ch006

Chen, Stephen. 2017. "Chinese nanny caught abusing baby sparks debate on domestic help in China." *South China Morning Post*, July 12. Accessed May 30, 2018. http://www.scmp.com/news/china/society/article/2102296/alleged-case-nanny-abusing-child-reopens-debate-about-domestic

Chen, Yi-Fan, and James E. Katz. 2009. "Extending family to school life: College students' use of the mobile phone." *International Journal of Human-Computer Studies* 67 (2): 179–191. doi:10.1016/j.ijhcs.2008.09.002

Deleuze, Gilles, and Félix Guattari. 1987. *A Thousand Plateaus: Capitalism and Schizophrenia*. Minneapolis: University of Minnesota Press.

Google Play, Family GPS Tracker and Chat + Baby Monitor Online. n.d. Accessed May 30, 2018. https://play.google.com/store/apps/details?id=gl.kid.alert&hl=en

Google Play, Find my Kids: Child Locator. n.d. Accessed May 30, 2018. https://play.google.com/store/apps/details?id=org.findmykids.app&hl=en

Hasinoff, Amy Adele. 2017. "Where are you? Location tracking and the promise of child safety." *Television & New Media* 18 (6): 496–512. doi:10.1177/1527476416680450

Hussain, Amir. 2016. "Maid jailed for abusing baby over his sleeping blues." *The Straits Times*, April 20. Accessed May 30, 2018. https://www.straitstimes.com/singapore/courts-crime/maid-jailed-for-abusing-baby-over-his-sleeping-blues

Katz, James E., and Mark A. Aakhus, eds. 2002. *Perpetual Contact: Mobile Communication, Private Talk, Public Performance.* Cambridge: Cambridge University Press.

Kelly, Lynne, Robert L. Duran, and Aimee E. Miller-Ott. 2017. "Helicopter parenting and cell-phone contact between parents and children in college." *Southern Communication Journal* 82 (2): 102–114. doi:10.1080/1041794X.2017.1310286

Lee, Ellie. 2014. "Introduction." In *Parenting Culture Studies*, edited by Ellie Lee, Jennie Bristow, Charlotte Faircloth, and Jan Macvarish, 1–24. UK: Palgrave Macmillan.

Lee, Soyoung, Peggy S. Meszaros, and Jan Colvin. 2009. "Cutting the wireless cord: College student cell phone use and attachment to parents." *Marriage & Family Review* 45 (6-8) 717–739. doi:10.1080/01494920903224277

Lim, Lee Ming, and Lim Sun Sun. 2015. "Entering adulthood: Mobile communication between parents and their emerging adult children." Paper presented at the Conference on Singapore Families and Population Dynamics, Centre for Family and Population Research, Singapore.

Lim, Sun Sun, and Becky Pham. 2016. "'If you are a foreigner in a foreign country, you stick together': Technologically mediated communication and acculturation of migrant students." *New Media & Society* 18 (10): 2171–2188. doi:10.1177/1461444816655612

Lim, Sun Sun, and Carol Soon. 2010. "The influence of social and cultural factors on mothers' domestication of household ICTs—Experiences of Chinese and Korean women." *Telematics and Informatics* 27 (3): 205–216. doi:10.1016/j.tele.2009.07.001

Longhurst, Robyn. 2013. "Stretching mothering: Gender, space and information communication technologies." *Hagar Studies in Culture, Policy and Identities* 11 (1): 121–138.

Lythcott-Haims, Julie. 2015. *How to Raise an Adult: Break Free of the Overparenting Trap and Prepare Your Kid for Success.* New York: Henry Holt.

Nelson, Margaret K. 2010. *Parenting out of Control: Anxious Parents in Uncertain Times.* New York: New York University Press.

Rutherford, Markella B. 2011. *Adult Supervision Required: Private Freedom and Public Constraints for Parents and Children.* Piscataway, NJ: Rutgers University Press.

Simpson, Brian. 2014. "Tracking children, constructing fear: GPS and the manufacture of family safety." *Information & Communications Technology Law* 23 (3): 273–285. doi:10.1080/13600834.2014.970377

Somers, Patricia, and Jim Settle. 2010. "The helicopter parent (Part 2): International arrivals and departures." *College and University* 86 (2): 2–9. Accessed March 10, 2019. http://www.aacrao.org/resources/publications/college-university-journal-(cu)

Tahnk, Jeana. 2013. "Apps to the rescue." *Scholastic Parent & Child Magazine*, August/September, 154–157.

Tan, Melissa. 2017. "11 things to note when choosing a preschool." *Smart Parents*, July 3. Accessed May 30, 2018. https://www.smartparents.sg/toddler/devt-and-milestones/11-things-to-note-when-choosing-a-preschool-8999652

theAsianparent Singapore. n.d. "4 tips on installing a CCTV at home to monitor your maid." *theAsianparent Singapore*. Accessed May 30, 2018. https://sg.theasianparent.com/monitor-the-maid-should-you-install-a-cctv-at-home-to-monitor/

The Straits Times. 2016. "New bus system will drive efficiency in school transport." *The Straits Times*, May 11. Accessed May 30, 2018. https://www.straitstimes.com/business/companies-markets/new-bus-system-will-drive-efficiency-in-school-transport.

Weisskirch, Robert S. 2009. "Parenting by cell phone: Parental monitoring of adolescents and family relations." *Journal of youth and adolescence* 38 (8): 1123. doi:10.1007/s10964-008-9374-8

Yang, Chia Chen. 2018. "Social media as more than a peer space: College freshmen encountering parents on Facebook." *Journal of Adolescent Research* 33 (4): 442–469. doi:10.1177/0743558416659750

Chapter 6

boyd, danah. 2008. "Why youth <3 social network sites: The role of networked publics in teenage social life." In *Youth, Identity, and Digital Media*, edited by David Buckingham, 119–142. Cambridge, MA: MIT Press.

Holloway, Sarah L., and Gill Valentine. 2000. "Spatiality and the new social studies of childhood." *Sociology* 34 (4): 763–783.

Howard, Jacqueline. 2017. "When kids get their first cell phones around the world." *CNN*, December 11. Accessed May 30, 2018. https://edition.cnn.com/2017/12/11/health/cell-phones-for-kids-parenting-without-borders-explainer-intl/index.html

Lim, Sun Sun. 2013. "Media and peer culture: Young people sharing norms and collective identities with and through media." In *Routledge Handbook of Children, Adolescents and Media*, edited by Dafna Lemish, 322–328. New York: Routledge.

Livingstone, Sonia, and Ellen J. Helsper. 2008. "Parental mediation of children's Internet use." *Journal of Broadcasting & Electronic Media* 52 (4): 581–599. doi:10.1080/08838150802437396

Rutherford, Markella B. 2011. *Adult Supervision Required: Private Freedom and Public Constraints for Parents and Children*. Piscataway, NJ: Rutgers University Press.

Simmons, Rachel. 2011. *Odd Girl Out: The Hidden Culture of Aggression in Girls*. Boston: Mariner Books.

Slonje, Robert, Peter K. Smith, and Ann Frisén. 2013. "The nature of cyberbullying, and strategies for prevention." *Computers in Human Behavior* 29 (1): 26–32. doi:10.1016/j.chb.2012.05.024

Wesch, Michael. 2009. "YouTube and you: Experiences of self-awareness in the context collapse of the recording webcam." *Explorations in Media Ecology* 8 (2): 19–34.

Whitten, Sarah. 2016. "Study: Kids are getting their first cell phone before they can drive." *CNBC*, May 20. Accessed May 30, 2018. https://www.cnbc.com/2016/05/20/study-kids-are-getting-their-first-cell-phone-before-they-can-drive.html

Winnicott, Donald Woods. 1990. *The Maturational Processes and the Facilitation Environment: Studies in the Theory of Emotional Development*. London: Hogarth Press.

Winnicott, Donald Woods. 2005. *Playing and Reality*. Oxford: Routledge Classics.

Chapter 7

Arnett, Jeffrey Jensen. 2004. *Emerging Adulthood: The Winding Road from the Late Teens through the Twenties*. New York: Oxford University Press.

Bandyopadhyay, Koyel. 2017. "Parents who are obsessed with social media are giving their kids an unhealthy complex." *Quartz*, April 26. Accessed May 30, 2018. https://qz.com/761953/parents-who-are-obsessed-with-social-media-are-giving-their-kids-an-unhealthy-complex/

Blackboard. 2018. "Trends in community engagement: Text, Twitter, email, call—new expectations for school-to-home communications." Accessed March 10, 2019. http://bbbb.blackboard.com/community-engagement-report

boyd, danah. 2008. "Why youth <3 social network sites: The role of networked publics in teenage social life." In *Youth, Identity, and Digital Media*, edited by David Buckingham, 119–142. Cambridge, MA: MIT Press.

Bray, Mark, and Chad Lykins. 2012. *Shadow Education: Private Supplementary Tutoring and Its Implications for Policy Makers in Asia*. The Philippines: Asian Development Bank.

Brown, Ivana. 2010. "Ambivalence of the Motherhood Experience." In *Twenty-first Century Motherhood: Experience, Identity, Policy, Agency*, edited by Andrea O'Reilly, 121–139. New York: Columbia University Press.

Budden, Beth. 2018. "Parents: Stop misusing class messaging apps." *Tes News*, September 16. Accessed March 10, 2019. https://www.tes.com/news/parents-stop-misusing-class-messaging-apps

Caronia, Letizia. 2008. "Growing up wireless: Being a parent and being a child in the age of mobile communication." In *Digital Literacy: Tools and Methodologies for*

Information Society, edited by Pier Cesare Rivoltella, 99–125. Hershey, PA: IGI Global. doi:10.4018/978-1-59904-798-0.ch006

Chao, Ruth, and Vivian Tseng. 2005. "Parenting of Asians." In *Handbook of Parenting: Volume 4: Social Conditions and Applied Parenting*, edited by Marc H. Bornstein, 59–94. New Jersey: Lawrence Erlbaum Associates.

Chao, Ruth K. 1995. "Chinese and European American cultural models of the self reflected in mothers' childrearing beliefs." *Ethos* 23: 328–354. doi:10.1525/eth.1995.23.3.02a00030

Chen, Fu-Mei, and Tom Luster. 2002. "Factors related to parenting practices in Taiwan." *Early Child Development and Care* 172 (5): 413–430. doi:10.1080/03004430214549

Cheng, Chung-tai. 2015. "The technologicalization of education in China: A case study of the home-school communication system." In *Social Robots from a Human Perspective*, edited by Jane Vincent, Sakari Taipale, Bartolomeo Sapio, Giuseppe Lugano, and Leopoldina Fortunati, 117–127. Switzerland: Springer.

Chung, Clarissa. 2016. "Enhancing safety of children." *The Star Online*, September 9. Accessed May 30, 2018. https://www.thestar.com.my/news/nation/2016/09/09/enhancing-safety-of-children-cctv-system-with-cloud-storage-to-monitor-nursery/

Clark, Lynn Schofield. 2013. *The Parent App: Understanding Families in the Digital Age*. New York: Oxford University Press.

Collins, Caitlyn. 2019. *Making Motherhood Work: How Women Manage Careers and Caregiving*. Princeton, NJ: Princeton University Press.

Deleuze, Gilles, and Félix Guattari. 1987. *A Thousand Plateaus: Capitalism and Schizophrenia*. Minneapolis: University of Minnesota Press.

EdTechReview. 2016. "Teno App—Changing the Way Schools in India Communicate with Parents." *EdTechReview*, June 20. Accessed May 30, 2018. http://edtechreview.in/trends-insights/trends/2412-teno-app-schools-india-communicate-parents

Fortunati, Leopoldina. 2002. "The mobile phone: Towards new categories and social relations." *Information, Communication & Society* 5 (4): 513–528. doi:10.1080/13691180208538803

Friedman, May. 2010. "It takes a (virtual) village: Mothering on the Internet." In *Twenty-first Century Motherhood: Experience, Identity, Policy, Agency*, edited by Andrea O'Reilly, 362–375. New York: Columbia University Press.

Furedi, Frank. 2002. *Culture of Fear: Risk-taking and the Morality of Low Expectation*. Revised edition. London: Continuum.

Furedi, Frank. 2008. *Paranoid Parenting: Why Ignoring the Experts May Be Best for Your Child*. London: Continuum.

Geinger, Freya, Michel Vandenbroeck, and Griet Roets. 2014. "Parenting as a performance: Parents as consumers and (de)constructors of mythic parenting and childhood ideals." *Childhood* 21 (4): 488–501. doi:10.1177/0907568213496657

Goldscheider, Frances, Eva Bernhardt, and Trude Lappegård. 2014. "Studies of Men's Involvement in the Family." *Journal of Family Issues* 35 (7): 879–890. doi:10.1177/0192513X14522237.

Heiman, Rachel, Mark Liechty, and Carla Freeman. 2012. "Introduction: Charting an anthropology of the middle-classes." In *The Global Middle Classes: Theorizing through Ethnography*, edited by Rachel Heiman, Carla Freeman, and Mark Liechty, 3–29. Santa Fe: SAR Press.

Henderson, Fiona. 2018. "WhatsApp? Parents are drowning in school info." *Tes News*, September 24. Accessed March 10, 2019. https://www.tes.com/news/whatsapp-parents-are-drowning-school-info

Hewlett, Sylvia Ann. 2007. "Is your extreme job killing you?" *Harvard Business Review*, August 22. Accessed May 30, 2018. https://hbr.org/2007/08/is-your-extreme-job-killing-yo

Ling, Rich. 2012. *Taken for Grantedness: The Embedding of Mobile Communication into Society*. Cambridge, MA: MIT Press.

Livingstone, Sonia, and Ellen J. Helsper. 2008. "Parental mediation of children's Internet use." *Journal of Broadcasting & Electronic Media* 52 (4): 581–599. doi:10.1080/08838150802437396

Lythcott-Haims, Julie. 2015. *How to Raise an Adult: Break Free of the Overparenting Trap and Prepare Your Kid for Success*. New York: Henry Holt and Company.

MacKenzie, Donald, and Judy Wajcman, eds. 1999. *The Social Shaping of Technology*. 2nd edition. Buckingham, UK: Open University Press.

Pleck, Joseph. 2010. "Paternal involvement: Revised conceptualization and theoretical linkages with child outcomes." In *The Role of Father in Child Development*, edited by Michael E. Lamb, 58–93. Hoboken, NJ: Wiley.

Sun, Yiting. 2016. "WeChat is extending China's school days well into the night." *MIT Technology Review*, March 8. Accessed May 30, 2018. https://www.technologyreview.com/s/600943/wechat-is-extending-chinas-school-days-well-into-the-night/

Tsuya, Noriko O., and Larry L. Bumpass, eds. 2004. *Marriage, Work, and Family Life in Comparative Perspective: Japan, South Korea, and the United States*. Honolulu: East-West Centre.

Tuoi Tre Online. 2018. "Lap camera lop mam non: 88% cha me dong y, 48% giao vien khong dong y." [Installing CCTVs in nursery schools and kindergartens: 88% of parents approved, 48% of teachers disapproved] *Tuoi Tre Online*, May 21. Accessed May 30, 2018. https://tuoitre.vn/lap-camera-lop-mam-non-88-cha-me-dong-y-52-giao-vien-khong-dong-y-20180521172030994.htm

Ungar, Michael. 2007. *Too Safe for Their Own Good: How Risk and Responsibility Help Teens Thrive*. Toronto: McClelland and Stewart.

Vietnamnet. 2017. "Tu 1/6, dua bang diem cua con len mang la pham luat." [Starting from June 1, parents' online posting of children's school reports will be against the law] *Vietnamnet*, May 28. Accessed May 30, 2018. http://vietnamnet.vn/vn/giao-duc/goc-phu-huynh/tu-ngay-1-6-dua-bang-diem-cua-con-len-mang-la-pham-luat-375243.html

Vygotsky, L. S. 1978. *Mind in Society: The Development of Higher Psychological Processes*. Cambridge, MA: Harvard University Press.

Wajcman, Judy. 2015. *Pressed for Time: The Acceleration of Life in Digital Capitalism*. Chicago: University of Chicago Press.

Winnicott, Donald Woods. 1990. *The Maturational Processes and the Facilitation Environment: Studies in the Theory of Emotional Development*. London: Hogarth Press.

Winnicott, Donald Woods. 2005. *Playing and Reality*. Oxford: Routledge Classics.

Yeung, Wei-Jun Jean. 2013. "Introduction: Asian fatherhood." *Journal of Family Issues* 34 (2): 143–160. doi:10.1177/0192513X12461133

Yeung, Wei-Jun Jean. 2016. "Fathers as caregivers." In *The Wiley Blackwell Encyclopedia for Family Studies*, edited by Constance L. Shehan, 1–5. Hoboken, NJ: John Wiley and Sons.

INDEX

Tables and figures are indicated by *t* and *b* following the page number

For the benefit of digital users, indexed terms that span two pages (e.g., 52–53) may, on occasion, appear on only one of those pages.